1966

SIX STUDIES IN QUARRELLING

VINCENT BROME

Six Studies in Quarrelling

*

CRESSET PRESS

1958

First published in 1958 by
the Cresset Press Ltd
11 Fitzroy Square, London W.1
and printed in Great Britain by the Shenval Press
London, Hertford and Harlow

Preface

THIS BOOK is primarily an entertainment. If it sets up deeper echoes, that clearly is all to the good. Certainly those involved had considerable depths of awareness and were passionately concerned about the great questions of their day. They were also supremely articulate. We have no equivalent of George Bernard Shaw, H. G. Wells, G. K. Chesterton, Hilaire Belloc and the indomitable Dr Coulton in the present age.

They grew up in an age 'when high-minded public men in broadcloth waved their countrymen towards a decorous millennium of cheap food and penny postage . . .,' as Philip Guedalla wrote. If enlightened values were difficult to detect amongst the increasing din of industrialization, the Poet Laureate, Mr Tennyson, still fell into lyrical raptures, and for those bothered by the troubles which beset the poor, there was always the robust invention of Mr Dickens to write another book about Mr Pickwick or Sam Weller, bursting with Victorian life. The fogbound capital, London, was the centre of the world. A considerable culture flowered and half-concealed the conflicts beneath the surfaces. The Fabian Society appeared in 1884 and the Independent Labour Party in 1893, both trying to convert into a conscious principle, forces which were then proceeding by blind instinct.

There were deep divisions within this society. Unflinching Christians fought desperately against the new Darwinians. Fabian young women tried to burst the suffocating bonds of sexual morality, the Fabians proper attacked capitalism, the workers were deeply divided against the employers, new young novelists challenged the place of literature in life, and even the drama was presently under siege from reckless young Socialists with

v

no conception of the niceties of dramatic subject or construction. More subtle divisions set the Catholics against the non-Catholics, the Socialists against the Marxists, and the scholars against literary historians.

From it all sprang prolonged quarrels and feuds, sometimes public, sometimes private, crystallizing the essence of a ferment which took place in the late Victorian era. This book isolates six such 'quarrels'. The key battle raged between Shaw and Wells, but Shaw clashed at length with Chesterton, Wells with Hilaire Belloc and Belloc with Dr Coulton. A whole series of exchanges between Wells, Henry Arthur Jones and Shaw became a fierce grapple. Later, Churchill turned speeches, articles and letters upon Wells who brilliantly hit back, and Henry James, beginning in gentle remonstrance, became very cross with the splenetic Wells. These and others represented not merely literary quarrelling and debate over months, sometimes years, at a high level of invective and eloquence; they were a great stimulus to modern thinking for the masses.

If it is not clear, it should be stated that these are only studies in the sense that the material itself reveals the nature of the men and their methods of quarrelling. In the first place I added extensive background detail, but careful examination revealed that much of this was implicit in the material itself and merely interfered with the sharp impact of attack and reply. Finally, I pared down background material to the essentials of the quarrels. It should also be confessed that it has been necessary to tear passages out of context in order to juxtapose attack and retaliation, and sometimes, the exact time sequence has been violated.

I have drawn on scores of letters, pamphlets, books, documents, some unpublished, some contained exclusively in the fine collection of G. K. Chesterton's executrix Miss Dorothy Collins, who generously made them available. Especially I am indebted to the late Edward Pease for many letters and reminiscences, to Miss Blanche Patch for a letter from Wells, to the Labour Party for an unpublished circular from Shaw. Some years before she died Dorothy Richardson also gave me invaluable material about these 'quarrels'. I acknowledge with thanks permission from The Public Trustee and The Society of Authors to quote from the letters and works of George Bernard Shaw, and from the Representatives of Henry James for permission to quote from his letters to Wells and others. Sir Winston Churchill also kindly permitted me to use quotations from articles he wrote in the *Sunday* and *Daily Express* in 1920. Hesketh Pearson generously made available material from his *Bernard Shaw—His Life and Personality*. Simon Nowell–Smith I must also thank for giving me access to the originals of certain letters of Henry James.

The executors of H. G. Wells, Henry Arthur Jones, Henry James, Hilaire Belloc, Dr G. G. Coulton and G. K. Chesterton have all very generously given me permission to quote from their works and letters, for which I am grateful. For the rest, the following publishers have been most helpful in granting permission to quote: Victor Gollancz Ltd and The Cresset Press from H. G. Wells' *Experiment in Autobiography*, Victor Gollancz Ltd from *The Life and Letters of H. A. Jones* by Doris Jones; Constable & Co Ltd from *The Legend of the Master* edited by Simon Nowell-Smith; Sheed and Ward Ltd from *A Companion to Mr Wells' Outline of History* and *Mr Belloc Still Objects* by Hilaire Belloc and *Gilbert Keith Chesterton* by Maisie Ward; *The New Statesman* from the *Stalin-Wells Talk*; Watts and Co from *Mr Belloc Objects* and *The Conquest of Time* by H. G. Wells; The Bodley Head from *George Bernard Shaw* by G. K. Chesterton; Collins from *Bernard Shaw—His Life and Personality* by Hesketh Pearson. The *Daily* and *Sunday Express* also kindly gave permission to quote from articles by H. G. Wells and Sir Winston Churchill. It remains to acknowledge the very considerable work of Miss J. Telford whose patience and skills were indispensable.

Contents

CHAPTER ONE

Shaw versus Wells

IT WAS the night of January 5, 1895, at the St James' Theatre, London. The row of dramatic critics in faultless evening dress was broken by one tall, red-whiskered man who wore an everyday brown jacket. Two seats from him sat a much shorter person discomfited by dress clothes which had been made at twenty-four hours' notice and by his sudden accession to the glories of dramatic criticism. When Cust, then editor of the *Pall Mall Gazette*, had asked H. G. Wells what he knew about the theatre, Wells replied that he had seen Henry Irving and Ellen Terry in *Romeo and Juliet* and Penley in the *Private Secretary*. 'Nothing else?' asked Cust. 'Nothing else,' replied Wells. 'Then you'll bring an entirely fresh mind to the theatre,' said Cust and thrust two pieces of coloured paper into his hand.[1] The play was Henry James' *Guy Domville* and George Alexander took the lead with refined solemnity throughout the first two acts. In the third, hostility from the audience brought a note of desperation into his voice.

As the curtain fell, Alexander, moved by an impulse which might have been revenge, led a doomed James, still unaware of precisely what this variety of noises registered, to the middle of the stage. James bowed, the gallery poured boos and cat-calls on his head, James went white, his mouth opening and shutting soundlessly, and then Alexander pulled him back into the wings.[2]

Simultaneously Wells noticed the red-bearded figure of Bernard Shaw rise from his seat and make towards the door. Immediately H. G. Wells followed. This was their first meeting. Shaw, at thirty-eight, was ten years older than Wells, thin to the point of gauntness and very poor, but poverty was no

[1] *Bernard Shaw—His Life and Personality*, p. 249. Hesketh Pearson.
[2] *Experiment in Autobiography*, p. 536. H. G. Wells.

I

restraint on his grandiloquence. Wells had written *The Time Machine*, *The Stolen Bacillus*, *The Wonderful Visit* and *Select Conversations With an Uncle*—all to be published in that prolific year 1895—but had not yet achieved anything resembling the assurance of Shaw. They must have made an odd pair walking through the night. Wells short, with tiny hands and feet, a massive brow, eyes brimming with intelligence, and Shaw leonine, gaunt, his rich voice echoing down the street. Conversation drifted from the play to wider matters and many years later Wells wrote . . . '*He talked like an elder brother to me in that agreeable Dublin English of his. I liked him with a liking that has lasted a life-time. In those days he was just a brilliant essayist and critic and an exasperating speaker in Socialist gatherings. He had written some novels that no-one thought anything of and his plays were still a secret between himself and his God.*'[1]

The London in which they met was a London dominated by the figure of Queen Victoria steadily moving into mists of near divinity. Lord Salisbury, Arthur Balfour and the dapper figure of Joseph Chamberlain (rarely without a flower in his buttonhole) were bright stars in the political heavens. Some members of Her Majesty's Conservative Government were troubled by rumblings from thousands of workers dissatisfied with their lot, but the illusion of automatic progress towards greater prosperity still remained in far too many minds. The timeless scene of the rich, mid-Victorian period had given place to the more restless late Victorian, but there was never a car on the streets, the telephone still seemed like sorcery, tobacco was fourpence an ounce and whisky three shillings a bottle. Streets were gas-lit, the roads echoed to the clatter of horses' hoofs and women wore skirts reaching to the ground.

The years 1890–1900 were years of Empire. Kipling expressed the philosophy by which the ex-hardware merchant Joseph Chamberlain tried to live and rule. A tremendous gathering of empire potentates brought eleven colonial prime

[1] *Experiment in Autobiography*, p. 539. H. G. Wells.

ministers into conference and there was much talk of a great
Empire Federation, while Queen Victoria reviewed a remarkable parade of Empire troops. But the message of Robert
Blatchford still had profound echoes and it was clear that too
much poverty and hardship was hidden away in the darkest
corners of Britain. Men and women in the trade unions, in local
government, the co-operative societies and the House of
Commons were part of a tide, slowly gathering tremendous
force, which was to bring about profound changes in fifty
years. If the people involved were largely unconscious of the
precise part they played, the tiny Fabian Society had appeared on
the scene with the intention of making them aware, gathering
new disciples in the process. Shaw threw off his challenge in
brilliant lectures—that the Working Class is Evil, Unnecessary
and Should be Abolished—To your Tents, O Israel, and Why
I Am Not An Imperialist.

It was in the Fabian Society that the relationship between
Shaw and Wells developed. Seven years after their first meeting
at the St James's Theatre, Graham Wallas and Shaw sponsored
Wells as a member of the Fabian Society, and the trouble
between them began.

'Trouble' is a misleading colloquialism which cannot possibly convey the Olympian volleying and thundering which
was to echo through literary England over the next half
century. Its beginnings may have lacked the splendours of later
days, but they quickly revealed that fire, eloquence and wit
which misled many into believing that these two were, from
the start, mortal enemies. Shaw was now a man in his forties,
married to a wealthy wife and a very important figure. Wells
had been described by W. T. Stead as a man of genius and a
row of brilliant scientific romances had culminated in *Kipps*
and *A Modern Utopia*. They were both atheists and Socialists,
they both regarded the invincible society about them as a dangerous muddle, but they carried themselves from the start with
what Wells described as a certain sustained defensiveness to-

3

wards one another. Wells' challenge to the Fabians and Bernard Shaw came to a head in 1906. He wrote to Mr Guest, a member of the Fabian Executive: '*Dear ill-treated Guest, I am having a go at the Fabians on January* 17.'

A paper, *Faults of the Fabians*, intended to shake their complacent gradualism, was already prepared and so successfully achieved its purpose as to bring the full wrath of the Society— Jovian when the joint thunderbolts of Shaw, Webb, Bland and Olivier were released at one stroke—down on his head. Wells delivered the paper personally: '*Mr Chairman and fellow Fabians*,' he began. . . . '*The trouble with this Society is that it is still half a drawing-room society lodged in an underground apartment or cellar with one secretary, one assistant and precious little else. . . . The first of the faults of the Fabian Society then, is that it is small, and the second that even for its smallness it is needlessly poor. . . .*

'*The task undertaken by the Fabians is nothing less than the alteration of the economic basis of the Society. Measure with your eye this little meeting, this little hall; look at that little stall of not very powerful tracts: think of the scattered members, one here, one there. . . . Then go out into the Strand. Note the size of the buildings and business places, note the glare of the advertisements, note the abundance of traffic and the multitude of people. . . . That is the world whose very foundations you are attempting to change. How does this little dribble of activities look then. . . .*'[1]

Wells continued—we have taken our motto from General Fabius and therein lies a major error. However successful the complacent gradualism of Fabius it led in the end to the obstruction of progress. Not Fabius but Scipio, the straight and direct fighter was the General they should model their methods upon. They needed to increase staff, add life and vision to their literature, multiply their income many times and then . . . '*Unless I am the most unsubstantial of dreamers such a propaganda as I am now putting before you ought to carry our numbers up towards ten thousand within a year or so of its commencement.*'

[1] *Faults of the Fabians*, read to the Society on February 9, 1906.

4

Wells' paper delighted the younger members of the society who at once demanded a re-examination of Fabian policy. The Old Guard—Shaw amongst them—agreed to appoint a Committee. Shaw tried to work with Wells over the next few months and later described the experience: '*With the single exception of myself, none of us could be described as perfect; and even with me Wells could not work. . . .*' Wells, Shaw said, admitted that there were three men in the movement of whom he unreservedly approved: Keir Hardie, Ramsay Macdonald and Philip Snowden. This was a proud day for the three; '*but let them not be too conceited about it. They have never tried working with Wells; I have. When they do try it, the verdict of the coroner's jury will be justifiable homicide, or else Keir and Mac will be hanged, and Snowden will see nothing but Wells' ghost, with two dirks sticking in it, for the rest of his life.*'[1]

Once the necessity for investigating Fabian policy was established Wells poured out letters in an attempt to get 'the right people' on the Committee. Many such letters went to Haden Guest. . . . Letter undated: '*We might have to have Keir Hardie up. He'd fill a place I could not. . . . I'm getting more and more sick of the way in which he keeps out of this affair. . . . Calmer is a damned fool and I don't care what he thinks. We are anti-Shaw. . . .*'

September 15, 1906: '*Coit's ratting off and doesn't want to sign. Go and tame him for God's sake. . . .*'

The Reform Committee at last drew up a report and the Executive prepared a reply. The report and the reply were discussed at several explosive sessions between 1906 and 1907. Red-haired, mercurial Haden Guest supported Wells, Webb with his eyes on the floor released his usual lisping cataract of information, Shaw, the smiling Mephistopheles, waited in the background, Bland in frock coat and monocle made impassioned pleas in the correct parliamentary manner and Wells —well according to Hesketh Pearson: '*Pressing his knuckles hard*

[1] *Pen Portraits and Reviews*, p. 296. Bernard Shaw.

on the table before him, addressing his tie, correcting himself frequently, losing the thread of his remarks, suddenly remembering a point, bursting into a long parenthesis and failing to get back to his main drift of thought, he droned and piped away in a wholly unimpressive manner. Conscious of his disadvantage, irritated with the Webbs ... he lost control of himself and made a personal matter of it, describing the Old Gang as liars, tricksters, intriguers, blackguards, reactionaries ... and all the other names invariably applied by one world-meliorist to other world-meliorists who have different plans for world melioration. ...[1]

It was to be expected that nothing so elementary as righteous indignation would overtake Shaw. He had by now perfected that crippling method of rejoinder which embraced every accusation made. ... They were all vain, he said; they all had their moments of spite, of becoming blackguards. '*It does not concern me that according to certain ethical systems all human beings fall into classes labelled liar, coward, thief and so on. I am myself according to these systems a liar, a coward, a thief, and a sensualist.*'[2]

It is commonly supposed that Shaw did no lobbying in the battle which followed and happily regarded the spectacle of Wells, bounding with immense skill through every propaganda manoeuvre, in ironic detachment. This is not true. An unpublished document written by Shaw and circulated to key members of the Fabians on December 11, 1906 said: '*May I urge you not to be absent from the adjourned meeting of the Fabian Society next Friday at Essex Hall at 7.30. I find that many members have not noticed that the amendment of Mr H. G. Wells on which a division will be taken is drawn up in such a manner that if carried it will act as an instruction to me and my colleagues on the Executive Committee ... to resign and not offer ourselves for re-election. Nothing but an overwhelming expression of opinion in a full meeting can avert the most serious consequences to the Society as the matter cannot*

[1] *Bernard Shaw—His Life and Personality*, p. 257. Hesketh Pearson.
[2] Ibid., p. 257.

be settled by a mere majority in a small meeting. I shall explain fully when I address the meeting. . . .'[1]

The crucial day arrived. Essex Hall, in the Strand, was filled to bursting point. Wells' battle with Shaw had widely publicised the little known Fabian Society and membership had increased enormously. Shaw formally moved a resolution to increase the Executive from fifteen to twenty-one, and Wells at once moved an amendment: *'To . . . substitute . . . "That this meeting approves the spirit and purport of the Report of the Committee of Enquiry and desires the outgoing Executive Committee to make the earliest possible arrangements for the election of a new Executive to give effect to that report".'*[2]

There was some question of Wells resigning if he did not get his way. Shaw plunged into the attack: *'This amendment of Mr Wells' is a flat instruction to the Executive to resign and not offer themselves for re-election* [heated dissent]. *I quite accept the protests of the framers of the amendment that this was not what they intended —it is clear enough by this time that they do not possess the art of saying what they mean. . . .'* [renewed protests].

Shaw pressed on to ask whether Wells intended to resign if defeated by the Fabian vote. Reassured by Wells that he had no such intention Shaw continued: *'That is a great relief to my mind—I can now pitch into Mr Wells without regard for the consequences.*

'Mr Wells in his speech complained of the long delay by the Old Gang in replying to his report. But the exact figures are: Wells ten months, the Old Gang six weeks. During his committee's deliberations he produced a book on America. And a very good book too. But while I was drafting our reply I produced a play. . . .'

Shaw paused, the audience cleared its throat, someone whispered, the pause became prolonged and the impossible seemed imminent. Could it be that the Master had revealed that commonplace weakness of losing the thread? Suddenly

[1] Document made available to me by Peter Willmott.
[2] *Fabian News,* December, 1906.

Shaw continued 'Ladies and Gentlemen—I paused there to enable Mr Wells to say—And a very good play too!'[1] Burst upon burst of laughter greeted this. Word of mouth evidence has it that Wells immediately answered 'And I did not take advantage of the pause because I knew Mr Shaw would not fail to tell you what a marvellous play he had written.'

Shaw pressed on: 'The Executive Committee has, throughout this movement, treated Mr Wells with studied consideration. We let his attack pass without a word only putting up Mr Webb to express our welcome of the inquiry and to say a few words in support. . . . We then allowed Mr Wells to nominate his committee absolutely as he chose. . . . I will not pretend that we were not a little taken aback when we found that we were to be excluded from his councils. The Executive treatment of Mr Wells has been throughout simply to let him have his way on everything. . . .'

Shaw's case steadily mounted in power and eloquence. This amendment he said must not be put. Wells had forced everyone into the extreme position where the present Executive must fall upon its collective sword in splendid suicide or Wells himself unconditionally surrender.

'I have had some difficulty in persuading my colleagues to consent to a withdrawal; but we feel that we cannot force friends like Mr Olivier and Mrs Reeves into the dilemma of having either to desert Mr Wells on the amendment, or vote for our ignominious expulsion. That is the situation: and I now leave Mr Wells to take what course seems right to him.'[2]

It threw the whole burden of a very complicated moral responsibility upon Wells. In the end the amendment was withdrawn. It did not prevent Wells from delighting Fabian groups, behind the scenes, with descriptions of the Old Guard. The Webbs he referred to as Donna Quixote and Sancho Panza, and Shaw—that intellectual eunuch—followed by homo sapiens gone to seed, the final result of overbreeding, a

[1] Bernard Shaw—His Life and Personality, p. 258. Hesketh Pearson.
[2] Fabian News, December, 1906.

sexless biped. Asked what sort of universe the Old Guard would create given a free hand he replied:

'... *They would take down all the trees and put up stamped tin green shades and sunlight accumulators....*' There would be '*admirable Webblets, mysteriously honest, brightly efficient, bright with the shine of varnish rather than the gleam of steel. One sees these necessary unavoidable servants of the workers' commonwealth —trusted servants, indispensable servants, in fact, authoritative and ruling servants—bustling virtuously about their carefully involved duties and occasionally raising a neatly rolled umbrella to check the careless course of some irregular citizen who had forgotten to button up his imagination or shave his character....*'[1]

Next came the battle for the re-formed Executive. Both sides put up candidates and Wells wrote once more to Haden Guest (letter undated): '*Looking forward to seeing you. It's quite lamentable your people have decided for the 21 Executive. It means that we shall either get Bland, Cecil and all that damned pack or we shall have to put up 16 or 18 strong condidates. We haven't got them....*' The back of the letter retailed, in neat handwriting, Wells' view of various candidates from Olivier and Mrs Reeves (safe) E. C. (Bad—Mediocre stuff) to Mrs Y (Very bad—absolutely untrustworthy—great friend of the Webbs and Shaws).

The election which followed gave Wells fourth place on the Executive accompanied by a number of friends, but it was still an Executive dominated by the people he had sought to remove. Both Shaw and Wells later gave their different versions of the Fabian episode. Shaw said that Wells cost him literally over £1,000 in hard cash by wasting his time. Just look at the demands he made he said: first that the normal order of a public meeting should be abolished; second that he himself should simultaneously achieve the role of chairman and speaker whenever he spoke; third that the Fabian Society should not merely censure but pour contempt on the heads of its executive com-

[1] *Bernard Shaw—His Life and Personality,* pp. 258-9. Hesketh Pearson.

9

mittee *'in order that its old leaders should be compelled to resign and leave Wells sole Fabian Emperor'*. Anyone else, Shaw said, would have been ignominiously thrown out of the Society at this point. Wells instead *'was humbly asked to withdraw his demands as it was not convenient just then to serve him up Sidney Webb's head on a charger'*. Rewarding Wells for the great condescension he had shown in complying, *'he was elected to the executive committee nearly at the top of the poll; and I, because I had been the spokesman of our deprecation of the vote of contempt— selected for that job because it was known that I liked him and would let him down easily—was reproached for my brutality to the Society's darling. . . .'*[1]

As for Wells, a phenomenal bout of humility produced this remarkable statement: *'On various occasions in my life it has been borne in on me, in spite of a stout internal defence, that I can be quite remarkably silly and inept; but no part of my career rankles so acutely in my memory with the conviction of bad judgment, gusty impulse and real inexcusable vanity, as that storm in a Fabian tea-cup. From the first my motives were misunderstood, and it should have been my business to make them understandable. I antagonized Shaw and Beatrice Webb . . . by my ill-aimed aggressiveness. . . .'*

Contrition became a little confused in the last sentences, as Wells' habit of infallibility took possession of him once more . . . *'I was fundamentally right and I was wrong-headed and I left the Society, at last, if possible, more . . . ineffective than I found it.'*[2]

In 1910 Wells moved to his new house, Easton Glebe, in the shadow of Dunmow. He was now forty-six. Middle age and sweeping success had given him a quite new verbal licence. In the years 1912–18 he took on all comers and he didn't mind who or what they were. Work continued apace. Sometimes he started at nine in the morning behind sound-proof doors and no-one dared disturb him until lunch. In the afternoons he might walk and talk, and after tea work went on again until

[1] *Pen Portraits and Reviews*, p. 295. Bernard Shaw.
[2] *Experiment in Autobiography*, p. 661. H. G. Wells.

dinner. Shaw's daily routine was very different. Between 1910-12 Wells produced *The History of Mr Polly*, *The New Machiavelli*, *The Country of the Blind and Other Stories*, *Floor Games* and *Marriage*.

For his part, Shaw, at fifty-six, had lately published *The Doctor's Dilemma* and the *Showing-up of Blanco Posnet* and in 1911 was to complete *Fanny's First Play*. A whole row of plays was in process of conception and the beautiful shorthand filled hundreds of pages as he poured words, ideas, dialogue to paper. He seemed, if anything, rather younger than ten years before, although his beard had whitening strands among the flaming red, and the year 1912 concentrated a number of trials and hardships which distressed him more than was apparent to the public eye.

Wells' new house, Easton Glebe, became the scene of the famous week-ends in the shadow of Dunmow when the Olympian figures of literature, biked, rode and walked to join issue on matters of cosmic consequence in between the ball game in the barn and the most elaborate charades. In certain moods games were almost as much the stuff of life to Wells as talking. He would persuade the most august figures to join in and it was a considerable spectacle to see Lord Olivier, G. K. Chesterton and even, on occasion, George Bernard Shaw, bursting about the barn smacking a rubber ball with an approximation to excitement.

There were 'exchanges' in the barn which passed from hand to mouth in gossip and reminiscence. Shaw, of course, loathed games, but the late Dorothy Richardson told me of one encounter between Wells and Shaw in which something like the following talk took place while they smacked the ball at one another in the barn. 'Shall—I ever' (whack) 'qualify for your Utopia, H.G.?' Shaw asked. 'Never' (whack) Wells replied. Shaw: 'And—' (whack) 'What will be your role in it?' Wells: 'If your conceit' (whack—laughter) 'hadn't already stolen the job—Emperor!'

At the end of an inordinately short game, Shaw—exhausted—
was said to have commented: 'If I had known my dear H.G. I
would have stayed at home. A strenuous sit down is my only
form of exercise.' Upon which Wells said: 'Incorrigible! Shaw
the Old Pretender—Just like Henry James. But I've recast that
dreary cliché for you. Shaw the first, Shaw the second and
P-Shaw! the public noise. . . .'

Rarely have two literary giants understood and so elaborately
practised that ferocity of friendship which permits blistering
abuse to accompany considerable warmth of feeling. When
Shaw described Wells' *Utopia* as a half-breed pretence masquer-
ading as serious social thinking, Wells at once replied that it was
so much better than an Irishman pretending to be a half-baked
English Voltaire. Letters, which were addressed '*My dear G.B.S.*'
and '*My dear H.G.*' sometimes ended '*Get into print and I'll punch
your head.*' At least one from Shaw began—'*Such a mighty smiter
excites my deepest devotion. . . .*' and Wells would sign himself
'*Affectionately H.G.*'

The 1914–18 war broke into the life of Easton Glebe with explosive results and carried Wells away on a wave of excitement
rather more eloquent than usual. If he adopted, in the beginning,
what was called the average liberal view, he quickly fell into the
fiercest patriotic attitudes, but he saw the war as something
much more than a struggle between France, Germany and
Britain. Dependent on the way in which we waged war and the
ultimate principles involved, this might carry us over into a
world where war, as a means of settling international disputes,
became unknown. Shaw went as eloquently in the opposite
direction. He took train to the Hydro Hotel, Torquay, and began writing a manifesto on the causes of war which quickly became highly personal: '*I felt as if I were witnessing an engagement
between two pirate fleets with, however, the very important qualification that as I and my family and friends were on board British ships, I
did not intend the British section to be defeated if I could help it. All the
ensigns were Jolly Rogers; but mine was clearly the one with the*

Union Jack in the corner. . . . You may demand moral courage from me to any extent, but when you start shooting and knocking one another about I claim the coward's privilege and take refuge under my bed. My life is far too valuable to be machine gunned.'[1]

The war was less than six months old when Wells wrote an article in the *Daily Chronicle*—The Future of Northern Europe —assessing what role Finland, Norway and Sweden might play. Passing reference to Shaw's muddle-headedness brought this letter dated December 23, 1914, post-haste from Shaw.

'There is a point at which Mr Wells' mind gives way. There are two symptoms. One of them is the now familiar and apparently inevitable English symptom of this kind of breakdown; a sudden and unprovoked attack on me. Mr Wells, without a word of warning, calls me muddle-headed. Muddle-headed!! Me! Bernard Shaw! the man whose clarity England can often hardly bear! I ask you—! Well no matter. The other is the introduction of a sacrificial lamb caught by the horns, a spectacle repugnant to zoology and abhorrent to Scripture.

'Let me turn the blinding ray of my wantonly disparaged intellect on this question of Finland and Russia. . . .' Look at this stuff about Germany offering Sweden part of Finland—why—*'the Swedes would not take Finland if it were given away to them with a pound of tea.'*

This was no Shavian invention but an actual Swedish utterance, Shaw said. No Swede would willingly undertake the burden of fortifying the Finnish frontier against Russia *'for the sake of a race which, though justly proud of its relatively high civilization has a large and to its immediate neighbours . . . rather unpopular share of the wealth which inequalities in civilization produce.'*

Mr Wells so much abhorred the whole Potsdam theory of life and took so little interest in official diplomacies which, at root, were largely responsible for the war, that *'he has never once alluded to them in the series of very inspiring and illuminating articles which the war has elicited from him'*.

---

[1] *Bernard Shaw—His Life and Personality*, p. 324. Hesketh Pearson.

Wells replied by letter within a week. It is worth quoting at some length:

'*It is impossible to ignore Mr Shaw and there can be little doubt that he is doing a great deal of mischief at the present time.* . . . *I have been quite exceptionally and generously disposed to take him seriously and find out what he amounts to, and this is what I find he amounts to. He is an activity, a restless passion for attention. Behind that is a kind of jackdaw's hoard of other people's notions; much from Samuel Butler, scraps of pseudo-philosophical phraseology such as that Life Force phrase he got from Dr Guest; old Hammersmith economics, worn fragments of Herbert Spencer, some Nietzsche conveyed no doubt from the convenient handbook of Mr Orage, shreds of theosophy, current superstitions, sweepings of all sorts of "advanced" rubbish but nothing anywhere of which one can say "Here is the thought of a man". And it is just this incoherent emptiness, combined with an amazing knack of fluent inexactitude which gives him his advantage in irresponsible attack, and which from his early repute as the Terror of the Fabian Society, has spread his vague and unsubstantial fame about the globe, far beyond the range to which even his . . . intellectual forces would have taken it.* . . .

'*The first thing he does almost invariably in his controversies, if one may give his displays so dignified a name, is to create a serio-comic atmosphere, the Shavian atmosphere, by wild boasting about his mental clarity and facetious abuse of his antagonist. My mind he declares is "giving way" and so on. At this the well trained Fabian spinster smiles almost maternally and prepares for the next phase of the "intellectual treat". This is a carefully untruthful statement of the antagonist's position. I say "carefully untruthful"; he does not err, he deliberately distorts. In this instance he declares that I think that Germany is holding out Finland as a bait to Sweden and so on. It is nothing to Mr Shaw that I did not suggest anything of the kind; the glib falsehood is necessary in this case and he utters it with as light a conscience as if, instead of offering rubbish as international politics, he was introducing a panacea at a fair.* . . .

'*In regard to this Russian business I am supposed to be in a state of bellicose enthusiasm; this is supposed to make me eager to secure and fix the Russian alliance at any cost, and so I toady to the Tsardom, with favourable lies about Russia, and generally behave like a scoundrel, to forward these high aims. . . .'*[1]

Clearly Shaw, continued Wells, had no ideas of his own, was incapable of normal thought, and failed to grasp the elementary fact that one could be concerned about truth in itself and express ideas for their own sake. . . . *'He thinks all utterances are calculated, tactical statements; he thinks one expresses ideas for an end, in order to annoy somebody, or to get somebody to do something; under every statement he looks for a motive; he is like those exasperating women who are always crying out "Ah I know why you said that". . . .'*

Battle was now unmistakably joined. Shaw had completed the pamphlet—*Common Sense About War*—which, among other things, suggested that the violation of Belgian neutrality amounted to nothing more than a device to excuse British intervention; that the soldiers of the opposing armies should shoot their officers and return home; that the English were known abroad as hypocrites; that abuse of the enemy, accompanied by paeans of self-praise, was not the most effective way of winning a war; that the lying official case against Germany was weaker than the true one. Of course it said a great many more far more sensible things, but Wells commented: *'Mr Shaw is one of those perpetual children who live in a dream of make believe and the make believe of Mr Shaw is that he is a person of incredible wisdom and subtlety running the world. . . . All through the war we shall have the Shavian accompaniment going on, like an idiot-child screaming in a hospital, distorting, discrediting, confusing, and at the end, when it is all over, we shall have voluminous pamphlets and prefaces explaining how modestly and dexterously he settled the Prussian hegemony and re-arranged Europe.'*[2]

It was the special gift of H. G. Wells that his storms evaporated quicker than the morning dew. He could launch a fierce attack on a well-known person one day and greet him with an

[1] *The full version of the correspondence between Shaw and Wells is under preparation by Professor Gordon Ray.*
[2] *Daily Chronicle*, December 30, 1914.

15

uncomfortable grin and an out-thrust hand the next. Shaw felt these last attacks very nearly justified him in punching Wells' head but he later wrote—'*there was no malice in them*'—and now, when they met again, momentary unease quickly gave place to avid conversation. Neither could resist the challenge to verbal duelling and once launched into it, all previous quarrels vanished.

Presently both Shaw and Wells clashed with Henry Arthur Jones and what followed not merely undermined Jones' belief in the Divinity but led into a quarrel with so many explosions that it justifies a separate chapter. Sufficient for the moment to say that Shaw found himself in temporary alliance with Wells, a spectacle seldom publicly prolonged.

Inevitably, by now, both men were absorbed in the results of that gigantic upheaval in human affairs, the Russian revolution, and both steadfastly refused to be swept away by the tide of revulsion which referred to 'Reds', 'beasts' and 'murderers' with synonymous intent. The visionary in H. G. Wells was beside himself with a scene where elements of the sordid and noble, brutal and generous, the repressive and planned threw up that tremendous heat and glare which always fired his imagination.

Under its powerful spell he set off for Russia in 1920 to find out what the revolution really amounted to. He saw what he described as a ramshackle civilization shattered by misgovernment and '*six years of war strain*'. He saw things which depressed and inspired him. He came upon the great bazaar markets of St Petersburg closed, shops with broken windows and little stock, roads eaten into by the frost and hundreds of poorly dressed people hurrying to and fro, carrying bundles. He found that many people had left the cities and tried to go back to the land, so that the population of St Petersburg had fallen by half a million. He found cities where inflation had reached high levels. But heroic attempts to control the situation were being made and somewhere a creative effort stirred within the confusion. He disbelieved in their faith, he laughed at Marx, but he under-

stood and tried to respect their spirit. A great part of their energies had been taken up with blockades, invasions, raids and the
attempt to keep Russia alive in the war, and one must not expect too much too quickly. Never was there such an amateurish
government, but it had succeeded in achieving an admirable
system of rationing and—to his own very considerable aston-
ishment—education seemed to be developing on reasonable
lines. There were also some liberally-minded men amongst the
Bolsheviks, men in whom he found a gleam of hope. Lenin for
instance. He met Lenin in Russia and described him as a short
man like himself, with a pleasant face and a torrent of talk. A
visionary, prepared to sweep away whole towns if they interfered with the master plan, Lenin spoke of the electrification of
Russia which would set an enormous pulse beating in the remotest
steppe, until Wells was almost persuaded that it could happen.

Wells came away a divided man. Lenin impressed him and it
seemed to him that something worthwhile might yet emerge
under his direction from the chaos. But huge divisions of people
into proletariat and bourgeoisie were still nonsense to Wells,
and he continued to find *Das Kapital* '*a monument of pretentious
pedantry*'.

Returning to England he fell into political argument with
Shaw. There were many exchanges, some in the Reform Club,
some over dinner with Keynes or Chesterton, and some by
letter. Shaw simply rocketed with laughter when he read what
Wells was alleged to have seen in Russia. Of course, everyone
knew that our dear H.G. was still living in the pink mists of his
Utopia, and remained incapable of understanding that considerable confusion, extending over a number of years, was the
inevitable concomitant of such a gigantic upheaval.

Wells made many prolonged and serious statements about
his visit. The chapter headings of his book, *Russia in the Shadows*
were revealing: 'Petersburg in Collapse'—'Drift and Salvage'—
'The Quintessence of Bolshevism'—'The Creative Effort in Russia'—'The Dreamer in the Kremlin'. There were also many arti-

17

cles in the British and American press. He later remarked that at this time there were few signs of the ruthless power-struggle which was to vitiate the hierarchy of the Communist Party itself and to reduce it, in the eyes of the Western world, to what we regarded as 'political thuggery'. In Wells' current writings, among whole pages with which Shaw violently disagreed, there was one passage which delighted him: '*In Russia I must confess my passive objection to Marx has changed to a very active hostility. Wherever we went we encountered busts, portraits, statues of Marx. About two-thirds of the face of Marx is beard, a vast solemn woolly uneventful beard that must have made all normal exercise impossible. It is not the sort of beard that happens to a man, it is a beard cultivated, cherished and thrust patriarchally upon the world. It is exactly like* Das Kapital *in its inane abundance. . . . A gnawing desire grew upon me to see Karl Marx shaved. Some day, if I am spared, I will take up shears and a razor against* Das Kapital*; I will write—* The Shaving of Karl Marx. . . .*'*[1]

Shaw said that being so hopelessly hairless himself, Wells' longing to shave the beard of Marx was obviously destructive envy. To Edward Pease he commented: 'My own beard is so like a tuft of blanched grass that pet animals have been known to nibble at it and then turn away in disgust . . . but it does not win me the same reverence as Marx.'

When a reporter called upon Mr Shaw to ask him whether he thought Mr Wells had any real knowledge of Marxism, he took down a copy of Wells' book, *Russia in the Shadows*, and turned to page 71 which said: '*When I was a boy of fourteen I was a complete Marxist long before I had heard the name of Marx. I had been cut off abruptly from education, caught in a detestable shop and I was being broken into a life of mean and dreary toil. I was worked too hard and for such long hours that all thoughts of self-improvement seemed hopeless. I would have set fire to that place if I had not been convinced it was over-insured.*'[2]

[1] *Russia in the Shadows,* pp. 69–70. H. G. Wells.
[2] Ibid., p. 72.

'So you see', said Shaw, 'Wells was a Marxist then and isn't now, which represents the usual brilliant flux of his mind.'

In the welter of witty and serious statements which Shaw made, his politics suffered some confusion. Early in the nineteen hundreds he had said that Socialism meant equal incomes for everyone since it was quite impossible to estimate the worth of an individual in terms of money. But Shaw had no illusions about money. '*All the thoughtful ones will assure you that happiness and unhappiness are constitutional and have nothing to do with money.*' On the other hand he was quite convinced that mal-nourished street urchins were produced by slums and not by original sin. He wanted the basic industries and services nation-alized, but he was very clear that nothing in private hands must be taken over, until public hands were quite ready to manage and run whatever had to surrender. Pressed hard enough, he confessed that his political creed was Modern Marxist Commun-ism. Some British Socialists recoiled in distaste from any such statement. Distaste gave place to horror when, speaking of the Russian revolution, Shaw bluntly announced: 'We are Socia-lists; the Russian side is our side.'

If this stunned some of his opponents to shocked silence, he hardly expected such a reaction from Wells. Yet Shaw resisted the idea that local Fabian branches should become outposts of the Russian revolution, and when a group of young Commun-ists outvoted him as Fabian delegate on a Research Committee, he resigned with an alacrity slightly indecent in a professed Marxist. He insisted that the Fabians had made a scientific study of Socialism which went beyond Marx and wanted British Socialism to be characteristically British.

Wells' Socialism was a curious hybrid which varied over the years but never quite eliminated the idea of a voluntary nobility ruling the world subject to special systems of recruitment and renewal. In his Utopia men were divided into four classes—The Samurai, the Poietic, the Kinetic, the Dull and the Base. The Samurai were a voluntary nobility who served their fellows with disinterested devotion; the Poietic represented the creative class capable of sustained attempts at pushing back the boundaries of knowledge and exploring new worlds; the Kinetic were the intelligent mass able to work within accepted formulas; and the Dull and Base were just the Dull and Base. There was to be considerable class mobility, members of any one class, excluding the Dull and the Base, qualifying for another, without regard for wealth, accent or creed. Much of the means of production was communally owned with certain relaxations for limited private property.

Time and again these issues set off explosions between Shaw and Wells, but the key political debate was sensibly delayed for a number of years.

It has been said that Wells brought the Modern Word down from the Rational Mountain with enormous fire and eloquence. He suffered personally what he wrote: he was part of the social upheavals which changed his world and he could speak with the authentic voice of one of the people, raised to a tenth pitch. Shaw remained the debonair spectator always detached from the experiences he described. If that hopelessly over simplified two such complex characters it was now very difficult to measure the comparative impact of their messages on the outer world. Millions of people went to Shaw's plays and came away seething with the kind of ferment he delighted to create; millions read Wells' far more sober-sided books and turned away sometimes moved, sometimes thoughtful, always stimulated.

Both were now popular oracles. Whatever they said was news. Living in a fierce limelight they issued judgments on kings and dictators, prime ministers, prelates, and divinities and one another. At £80 a thousand words they told humanity in the great national newspapers that it was a sordid mess.

Whenever they met and fell into debate, their respective methods were dazzling to watch. Shaw's Irish brogue, interrupted by gusts of laughter, poured relentlessly on, sometimes enlivened by enormous oaths, sometimes emphasized by hand-rubbing and great sweeps of the arm. Enlivening everything he said was a gaiety and charm which enabled his opponents to suffer destruction at his hands without feeling it too much. Incurably restless, he jumped up and down from his chair, crossed and uncrossed his legs, pushing his hands in and out of his pockets, talking and gesticulating in full spate. His tall, very upright figure literally crackled with energy.

Equally restless, Wells' gestures too were torrential, but his capacity for gay and vivid argument easily collapsed into that quarrelling which Shaw so adroitly avoided. If there was, at the beginning of their debates, some sense of a satellite winking and sparking around Shaw, flashes of a quite brilliant kind from Wells quickly made it impossible to say which was star and which satellite. Given the merest hint of a subject both could instantly talk at the length of a book, and there were occasions when the clash of their simultaneous talk ran on, oblivious of one another.

Within their respective messages they split most violently on science and fell to bickering in the nineteen twenties.

Wells later wrote: '*In conversational intercourse a man's conclusions are of less importance than his training and the way he gets to them, and in this respect chasms of difference yawned between Shaw and myself. . . . To him, I guess, I have always appeared heavily and sometimes formidably facty and close-set; to me his judgments, arrived at by feeling and expression, have always had a flimsiness. I want to get hold of Fact, strip off unessentials and, if she behaves badly put her in stays and irons; but Shaw dances round her and weaves a wilful veil of confident assurances about her as her true presentiment.*'[1]

Shaw commented: '*Imposter for imposter; I prefer the mystic to the scientist—the man who at least has the decency to call his nonsense a mystery, to him who pretends that it is ascertained, weighed, measured, analysed fact. . . . There is nothing that people will not believe nowadays if only it be presented to them as science and nothing they will not disbelieve if it be presented to them as religion. I myself*

[1] *Experiment in Autobiography*, p. 540. H. G. Wells.

began like that; and I am now receiving every scientific statement with dour suspicion whilst giving very respectful consideration to the inspirations and revelations of the poets and prophets. . . .'

There followed the long raking cross-fire on vivisection which presently involved some fixed stars in the scientific heavens and delighted the hearts of both sides convinced that their respective champions had won. Wells first posed the question—what is vivisection?—and answered: *'It is a clumsy and misleading name for experimentation on animals for the sake of the knowledge to be gained thereby. It is clumsy and misleading because it means, literally, "cutting up alive", and trails with it to most uninstructed minds a suggestion of highly sensitive creatures, bound and helpless, being slowly anatomized to death. This is an idea naturally repulsive to gentle and kindly spirits, and it puts an imputation of extreme cruelty on vivisection which warps the discussion from the outset. . . .'*[1]

With no sign of irascibility Wells poured on to say that the majority of experiments upon animals involved very little pain. Discomfort rather than actual pain might overtake an animal, and if the prick of an injection was followed by something resembling an illness, whenever cutting took place anaesthetics were used and in *'a considerable proportion of such cases there is no need for the animal to recover consciousness and it does not recover consciousness'.*[2]

Ignoring, for the moment, the implications of 'a considerable proportion' Shaw wrote: *'We have it at last from Mr Wells. The vivisector experiments because he wants to know. On the question whether it is right to hurt any living creature for the sake of knowledge, his answer is that knowledge is so supremely important that for its sake there is nothing it is not right to do.*[3] *Thus we learn from Mr Wells that the vivisector is distinguished from the ordinary run of limited scoundrels by being an infinite scoundrel. The common*

[1] *Sunday Express*, July 24, 1927.
[2] Ibid.
[3] *Shaw on Vivisection*, p. 32.

scoundrel who does not care what pain he (or she) inflicts as long as he can get money by it, can be satiated. With public opinion and a stiff criminal code against him he can be brought to a point at which he does not consider another five pound note worth the risk of garrotting or sandbagging or swindling anybody to get it. But the vivisector scoundrel has no limits at all except that of his . . . own mental capacity for devising them.[1]

Answering Shaw's facts, Wells believed, was one thing; answering his exaggerations quite another. As to his facts . . . '*The medical profession massively supports vivisection and its testimony is that the knowledge derived from vivisection has made possible the successful treatment of many cases of human suffering. . . . So far as we can measure one pain against another, or the pain of this creature against the pain of that, vivisection has diminished the pain of the world very considerably. But Shaw will hear nothing of this. . . .*'[2] Wells ran on for many magnificent sentences. '*Admittedly a small residue of cases remain in which real suffering is inflicted, but this is infinitesimal beside the gross aggregate of pain inflicted day by day upon sentient creatures by mankind. . . . Far more pain, terror and distress is inflicted on the first day of pheasant shooting every year for no purpose at all except the satisfaction of the guns.*'

Shaw now believed that to separate Wells' facts, exaggerations and opinions, was impossible because Wells mixed all three in some concoction called Wellsian wisdom. Take this stuff about pain caused to pheasants on the first day of pheasant shooting:

'*Clearly this, though valid as an indictment of pheasant shooting is no defence of vivisection.*' And take the residuum of painful cases being small in comparison with the gross aggregate of pain inflicted by mankind. . . . It was the kind of defence which could be made to fit a whole range of crime from pitch and toss to manslaughter, but not the simplest village constable was going to be taken in by such hocus-pocus. Shaw rolled on with one

[1] *Shaw on Vivisection*, pp. 32–33.
[2] *Sunday Express*, July 24, 1927.

C   23

splendid sentence after another, invoking the most unlikely people. . . .

'*Even Landru and the husband of the brides in the bath, though in desperate peril of the guillotine and gallows, had not the effrontery to say "It is true that we made our livelihood by marrying women and burning them in the stove or drowning them in the bath when we had spent their money; and we admit frankly and handsomely that the process may have involved some pain and disillusionment for them; but their sufferings (if any) were infinitesimal in comparison with the gross aggregate of pain inflicted day by day upon sentient creatures by mankind." Landru and Smith knew what Wells forgot: that scoundrels who have no better defence have no defence at all.*'

It was Wells' belief that reference to Landru and Smith was hopelessly irrelevant. Vivisection had a quite different and humanely dignified purpose. There was no gloating. Moreover, he, Wells, did not grant Smith or Landru, or any of those fellows, sufficient humanity even to acknowledge the existence of anaesthetics which would of course spoil their pleasure. Shaw, as usual, invoked a set of murderers to describe the activities of scientists but he would never think of invoking Darwin or Haldane to describe the activities of Landru or Smith. As for these other anti-vivisectionists—they would quite happily leave the abattoir intact while they forced the laboratory to close; they would recognize the right and duty of the owner of a dog to beat his unfortunate possession into good behaviour—but controlled, humanely conducted experiments for the sake of human welfare—No!

Shaw presently wrote: '*When a man says to society "May I torture my sister or her baby in pursuit of knowledge?" Society replies "No". If he pleads "What! Not even if I have a chance of finding out how to cure cancer by doing it?" Society still says "Not even then". If the scientist, making the best of his disappointment, goes on to ask may he torture a dog, the stupid and callous people who do not realize that a dog is a fellow creature, and sometimes a good friend, may say "Yes". But even those who say "You may torture a dog" never say "you may*

24

torture my *dog*" *and nobody says* "Yes! *because in the pursuit of knowledge you may do as you please.*" *Just as even the stupidest people would say* "If *you cannot attain to knowledge without boiling your mother you must do without knowledge*" *so the wisest people say* "If *you cannot attain knowledge without torturing a dog you must be literally a damned fool, incapable of putting knowledge to any use*".[1]

In 1928 Pavlov's book, *Conditioned Reflexes, an Investigation of the Physiological Activity of the Cerebral Cortex*, appeared.

'This', wrote Shaw, '*is an imposing title, but all it means is:* "Our *habits, How We Acquire Them and How Our Brains Operate them*".'

It was a book which brought an impassioned eulogy from Wells mounting steadily to a dramatic comparison.... If he '*stood on a pier in a storm with Shaw and Pavlov struggling in the waves*', Wells said, and he '*had only one lifebuoy to throw*', he '*would throw it to Pavlov and not to Shaw*'.[2]

This typical Wellsian extravagance encouraged Shaw to challenge Pavlov, Wells, Haldane, the biologists and geneticists all at one stroke. Pavlov he was especially concerned with because he had taken the unpardonable liberty of presenting such a resemblance to Shaw that their photographs were indistinguishable. Pavlov, Shaw said, had reached the pinnacle of scientific fame '*on the strength of his tissue of sham logic*', and it was astounding that it appeared to have imposed on such a brain as that of H. G. Wells. The truth, in fact, was that '*Pavlov's book is so unreadable after the first chapters ... I am apparently the only person who has ever read it right through from end to end. All the rest gave in before they came to the nonsense and the tortures*'.

Clearly Wells did not permit Shaw to get away with that. They debated, corresponded and analysed. According to the late Edward Pease they met on one occasion in the Reform Club and a conversation along the following lines took place:

Wells: You, Shaw, are the one who did not read Pavlov. You misread him.

[1] Preface to *The Doctor's Dilemma*.
[2] *Bernard Shaw—His Life and Personality*, p. 261. Hesketh Pearson.

25

Shaw: Did you or did you not say that Pavlov's dogs liked him?

Wells: Sometimes they liked him.

Shaw: While he was cutting half their brains out, piercing their cheeks to study their salivation?

Wells: During the experiments they were incapable of feeling since they were anaesthetized.

Shaw: And during the experiments Pavlov made the shattering discovery of such concern to international welfare that a dog's mouth watered when he heard the dinner bell.

Wells: Put in its biological perspective an epoch-making discovery which you will never understand.

Shaw: If the fellow had come to me I could have given him the same information in less than 30 seconds without tormenting a single dog.

Wells: But you don't even know the Behaviourist position—you don't understand that the mind is a system of reflexes held together by a body—that it is not an originally unified assembly whose factors have lost touch with each other. . . .

At this stage in Shaw's career H. G. Wells, Sir Almwroth Wright and J. B. S. Haldane agreed that discussing biology with Shaw was rather like discussing Newton with Ptolemy. Shaw claimed that he was a disciple of Haldane's father, Scott Haldane, who had led the movement to restore psychology to its predominance. Challenged on this Shaw immediately said:

'*What are you complaining about? I'm only showing you fellows the value of your own discoveries—Why allow me all the credit for them?*'

Wells regarded this as just another example of the well-known spectacle whereby Shaw won the argument and drowned the truth. Shaw, he said, was the kind of man who not merely permitted sentimentality to block the path of science, but was prepared to invert far too many truths in the interests of an activity to which his whole life was dedicated—phrase making.

There followed an episode which left Wells with a real sense of grievance and it was almost as if their close understanding of personal abuse broke down. Wells' wife Catherine, found to be suffering from cancer of the uterus, was given six months to live, and Wells later wrote . . . '*I had always expected to die before my wife and the shock I got was terrific. But this event released a queer accumulation of impulses in Shaw. He was impelled to write that this was all stuff and nonsense on the part of my wife and imply that she would be much to blame if she died. There was no such thing as cancer and so forth and so on.*'[1]

Wells regarded this as cruel. Among the chorus of approval commonly roused by Shaw's implacable good humour in debate it is curious to find not only Wells but Bertrand Russell saying that he could, on occasion, be very cruel. Certainly, Charlotte, Shaw's wife, was now moved to send a letter to Wells saying that he must not mind what her husband wrote. Wells should try not to be hurt by his tactlessness. Bernard had to do these things. She tried to prevent him and that was more and more her role as life went on.[2]

Catherine Wells' illness developed rapidly. Intolerable to those who loved and watched her, it was made bearable by morphine, as she wasted to impossible frailty. On Sunday, September 15, 1927, Arnold Bennett recorded in his journal: '*We drove down to Easton Glebe to see Jane Wells. Frank Wells was there with his fiancée, Peggy, and Gip with wife Marjorie. Jane was too ill to come down or see anyone. H.G. was visibly very much upset indeed.*'

She died shortly afterwards. At her own request she was cremated. Like a demon materializing beside the dead, Shaw went to the service and as the coffin slid towards the furnace doors he whispered to H.G. 'Take the boys and go behind; it's beautiful.'[3] Wells, so easily offended, so lately outraged by Shaw's letter, did not react with his normal fury. Indeed now, as Shaw added

[1] Obituary of Shaw written by Wells before Shaw's death and published in the *Daily Express*, November 3, 1950.
[2] Ibid.
[3] *The Book of Catherine Wells*, p. 42.

—'I saw my mother burnt there. You'll be glad if you go'—
Wells quietly took Shaw's advice, went behind, watched the
flames swarm over the coffin, and later wrote: '*It was good to
think she had gone as a spirit should go.*'[1]

Wells in his sixties was a dumpy, irascible little man still given
to vituperative eloquence, still capable of enchanting anyone
whenever he chose, and aware that middle age had made the
plump stomach, carried on two short legs and tiny feet, rather
too evident.

Shaw was even more gaunt and leonine, his red beard had
gone white, his face achieved a new austerity, but the diamond
twinkle in the eye, the great gusts of laughter and outpourings,
had increased rather than diminished.

As everyone knows, Shaw was vegetarian and Wells a hearty
meat eater. Shaw loathed sexual intercourse and never slept
with his wife or indulged sexually the innumerable women who
would willingly have sacrificed themselves to his lightest whim.
Wells, too, had abandoned sexual relations with his wife but
mistresses were the stuff of life to him, sending him spiralling to
his creative towers. Shaw lived a rigorous, organized life, dis-
daining normal indulgences. Herbert Wells, riding the moment's inspiration as it came, had an Elizabethan zest for every
appetite. Shaw loathed the games which so much delighted
Wells and H.G. could not understand why it was that when
Shaw invaded London he had to rise every morning before
breakfast and swim in the pool of the R.A.C. If both possessed
that gift of the Gods—torrents of nervous energy—Shaw's ani-
mation was more disciplined than Wells, who enjoyed no experience better than bursting his own banks to the delight of
his now innumerable disciples.

Both immensely mature personalities, their philosophies had
achieved a resolution very different from the days when Wells
wrote *First and Last Things*—now considered adolescent—and
Shaw wrote his early Fabian Essays. It would need volumes to

[1] *The Book of Catherine Wells*, p. 43.

28

interpret these philosophies, for if they remained Socialists and atheists, differences had developed of a fundamentally alien kind.

Wells saw himself as a temporary device of skin, bones, arteries and ganglia, a mysterious encasement of flesh and blood, involving consciousness and with certain things to do which no one else could do, but when they were done he would dissolve into dust, finished beyond any hope of resurrection. '*I shall serve my* biological *purpose,*' he wrote, '*and pass under the wheel and end. That distresses me not at all.*' Our personalities are '*serviceable synthetic illusions of continuity*'. '*Up and down the animal series,*' he said, '*the contribution of any individual to the life of the species is a trivial difference. Whether the new difference has immediate* survival value *or not is the sole criterion. If it has not, that individual is wiped out and there is an end to it.*'[1]

Shaw's belief in a Life Force took him into a World not so easily grasped, far less biological and—possibly—more optimistic. Wells derived from Darwin, Shaw from Lamarck, but Shaw accepted Butler's extension of Lamarck and carried it into what Wells regarded as metaphysical fields.

Conceivably, he said, the same power that has taken us thus far can take us farther. '*If* . . . *Man now fixes the term of his life at three score and ten years, he can equally fix it at three hundred, or three thousand.* . . . *This is not fantastic speculation; it is deductive biology, if there is such a science as biology.*'[2]

For Shaw, life's entry into and concern with matter was a temporary phase in man's development. Matter was 'entered into' in order that it might be transcended. In an attempt to enlighten what they pretended was their respective thick-headedness, Shaw and Wells clashed once more over the definitions involved in these two outlooks. It cannot be said that Wells at least found much enlightenment.

As he once said to Shaw in a moment of colloquial simplification: It all seemed to him a question of necks. Darwin believed

[1] *The Conquest of Time.* H. G. Wells.
[2] *Back To Methuselah.* G. B. Shaw.

that giraffes grew long necks *by chance* and survived. Lamarck believed an element of effort entered into growing long necks, and Butler, that some giraffes employed will power in their neck elongation, which added purpose to survival. He, Shaw, had swallowed Butler's extension of Lamarck only to disguise it under the meaningless title, Life Force.[1]

Shaw regarded this as appalling misrepresentation. He quoted Lilith from *Back to Methuselah* at Wells: '*I brought life into the whirlpool of force and compelled my enemy Matter to obey a living soul. . . .*'

Wells thought this so much verbiage explaining precisely nothing. Shaw wrote in the preface of *Back to Methuselah:* '*. . . The will to do anything can and does, at a certain pitch of intensity set up by conviction of its necessity, create and organize, new tissue to do it with. . . . If the weight lifter under the trivial stimulus of an athletic competition can "put up a muscle", it seems reasonable to believe that an equally earnest and convinced philosopher could "put up a brain". Both are directions of vitality to a certain end. Evolution shows us this direction of vitality doing all sorts of things. . . .*'[2]

Wells sizzled with a kind of mental anguish that anyone could be so romantically silly. This a Life Force! This invisible factor he could not anywhere detect in the blundering thrust of evolution, a Life Force—Nonsense! Look at it biologically. There was a thing called Survival Value which had little relation to any Life Force. '*There is much plausibility*', he wrote, '*in the theory that an astronomical shock spun the plane of the ecliptic away from the plane of the equator, split the equable Mesozoic year into four seasons, and so set a premium of survival value upon fur and feather, with their wider range, their need for seasonal adaptability and the enlarging brains which contributed to that adaptability. But so far these are mere theorizings. No alteration of the plane of the ecliptic will account for the extinction of the marine icthyosaurus, nor is there any satisfactory reason for such facts in the history of life as the dis-*

[1] Explained by Shaw to the present author.
[2] *Back to Methuselah*—Preface. Bernard Shaw.

appearance of the ammonites at the apex and end of the Mesozoic. Our knowledge of biological evolution is still only an outline studded with such riddles. . . .'[1]

This, to Shaw appeared equally irrelevant. He could not see what a jungle of biological illusion had to do with his clearly defined Life Force. He saw Man transcending matter to emerge at a quite different level of consciousness and Wells saw: *'Every living thing, every living particle . . . contributing to the career of life in space and time.'*[2] But *'Nature betrays no aesthetic preferences; glory, tragedy or burlesque, are all alike to her. There is little dignity in natural history. Most palaeontology is burlesque, a demonstration of the absurd. . . .'*[3]

Wells regarded Napoleon as a third rate adventurer in politics, Marx an imposter in sociology and Shaw a sentimental ignoramus in science. For his part the word science was liable to set Shaw rocketing with laughter. Science! that fabulous series of postulates purporting to explain what, in the last resort, it could not even see, thereby destroying its own empirical basis. Dear H.G. Did he really, in all sanity, compare that fumbling old woman to his beautiful Life Force? It was presently Wells' belief that if the argument went on much longer—*'Your Life Force will be the death of me.'*[4]

In 1930 Shaw invited Wells to a performance of *John Bull's Other Island* and in another unpublished letter Wells wrote:

'In spite of your disgusting caricature of me in Broadbent—even my slight tendency to embonpoint was brought in—I enjoyed John Bull's Other Island. . . .

'You're a great swell Shaw really—with something in your blood that ever and again breaks out in little blemishes of perversity. You have every element of greatness except a certain independence of your own intellectual excitability. You can't control your own wit and your

---

[1] *The Conquest of Time,* pp. 51–52. H. G. Wells.
[2] Ibid., p. 51. H. G. Wells.
[3] Ibid., p. 49.
[4] Verbal evidence to the author from G. B. Shaw.

love of larking. You ought to dull yourself with meat and then you'd be great. . . .[1]

In 1934 Wells travelled across Europe to visit Stalin in the Kremlin. The occasion was historic. A talk scheduled to last three-quarters of an hour lasted for three hours, perhaps because two men recited their own creeds with unflinching faithfulness, granting, as it were, suitable pauses for assimilation of those subtleties which each regarded as a little beyond the other.

At the outset they exchanged old world courtesies which seemed to belong to another generation but it quickly became apparent that their differences were wide. Wells was under the impression, he said, that the Roosevelt administration in America had brought about a much closer relationship between the ideas of Washington and Moscow. Stalin resisted any such proposition, but did not want to belittle the initiative, courage and determination of Roosevelt. America, he said, was attempting to modify and correct the economic structure of America in such a way as to maintain its identity and remove its dangers. Russia had entirely revolutionized her economy and given it a new basis.

Wells expressed his distaste for the labels applied by Marx—proletariat, bourgeoisie, emancipated intellectual—and said that it was no use appealing to the men he had in mind with such propaganda. Stalin admitted that men like Ford and Rockefeller had remarkable powers of organization but pointed out that even greater skills might be involved in organizing them.

Wells asked whether Stalin did not regard a great reform as a small revolution, implying that, given a sufficient number of great reforms spread over a generation, the result would be equivalent to a revolution with the inestimable advantage that the social fabric would not have been torn asunder. Stalin simply answered: 'The essence of reform is that the bourgeoisie grant concessions under the pressure of the lower classes in order to stay in power. Revolution means transference of power.'

[1]Letter kindly made available by Blanche Patch, Shaw's secretary.

It was really no good; no good at all. Both men emerged with their political philosophies completely intact. It was no use trying to persuade Stalin that—a self-elected elite, drawn from humanity as a whole, would penetrate the social confusion, appeal to man's rational instincts to become cosmopolitan citizens, and establish World Government without revolution. Nor was it possible to win Wells over to the belief that the class struggle must overthrow capitalism, establish the dictatorship of the proletariat and lead to a material millenium. Stalin as much scoffed at Wells' conviction that a planned economy imposed on the old capitalist system, beginning with the state control of heavy industries and banks, would lead to a Socialist state, as Wells resisted the chaos which went with physical violence and the simple acceptance of one unquestioned dogma. Stalin insisted that at root Western politicians were concerned with power, privilege, and staying-in-power, and no amount of liberalization would ever put power into the right hands; Wells instantaneously wondered which exactly were the right hands to hold power. And so it went on. . . . It would be out of place here to analyse their argument in any depth because I am concerned with Shaw and Wells and not with Stalin and Wells.

Wells returned to England. Newspapers made considerable play with his visit and presently a ferment began which brought this comment from Shaw: 'The conversation, or rather collision, between these two extraordinary men has not told us anything we did not know as to their respective views; but it is entertaining as a bit of comedy; and I suspect it was not lost as such on Stalin; for he is a man with a keen sense of comedy and a very ready and genial laugh. . . .

'Stalin listens attentively and seriously to Wells, taking in his pleadings exactly and always hitting the nail precisely on the head in his reply. Wells does not listen to Stalin; he only waits with suffering patience to begin when Stalin stops. He thinks he knows better than Stalin all that Stalin knows. He has not come to be instructed by Stalin but to instruct him. He is going to save the world by Clissoldism. He does not know that Clissold is only the moralized capitalist of

33

Comte, Comte being a back number because he had no better solution of the class war difficulty.'[1]

He even attempted, Shaw said, to put Stalin in what he conceived to be his place with the immortal words:

'*Perhaps I believe more strongly in the economic interpretation of politics than you do. . . .*'

Dear, dear H.G. He reproached Stalin, Shaw said, with attacking his Clissolds '*forgetting that Stalin has found it necessary to approach them . . . with a job in one hand and a gun in the other*'.

Whereupon H.G. declared that his Clissolds understood the world to be a bloody muddle but regarded his, Stalin's, class-war as nonsense. And so it continued.

Shaw would not go so far as to say that Wells appeared throughout the interview temporarily bereft of his hearing; but Robert Owen's famous dictum—never argue repeat your assertion—had seldom been practised with such perfection. Wells was a very good talker and the worst listener in the world. This was fortunate. '*For his vision is so wide and assured that the slightest contradiction throws him into a blind fury of contemptuous and eloquently vituperative impatience.*'

Asked to reply, Wells at once commented—Who can reply to Mr Bernard Shaw, a man practising '*the woman's privilege of wanton incoherent assertion. The torrent of fanciful misrepresentation and shrewd insinuation flows; one shrugs one's shoulders. I am Clissold, I am Ponderevo, I am anything but myself; I am mean, I am vain, no gentleman. If it makes Shaw happier so be it. He has said it all beautifully time after time. . . . But why did he repeat all this stuff about my personality when there were better things to write about? I had a conversation with Stalin and so did Shaw and Lady Astor, but I know of no official report of that encounter. I have only Stalin's remarks upon it and they are not for public use. . . .*'[2]

Wells said that he had never regarded Fabianism and its antagonist Marxism as '*the culmination of human wisdom*'. He, Wells,

[1] *New Statesman Pamphlet*, 1934.
[2] Ibid.

had moved with the times. He had steadily come to terms with contemporary facts, while Shaw continued to stick valiantly to his completely out-dated guns. . . . His, Wells', conception of a change of scale as the reality underlying contemporary affairs was pregnant with so many possibilities. It made this jumble of hates and misconceptions which constituted the class war as out of date as witchcraft.

Shaw would never understand these things. He, Wells, might be indisposed, as Shaw said, to listen to what he had heard before *but for all intellectual ends* [Shaw's] *touchily defensive egotism and his disposition to dramatize, make so brilliant a clamour that he is practically stone deaf'*. Beyond the clash of personalities the human mind was pressing on towards *'realizations of the vastest sort and this squabbling legacy from the ages of scarcity fades to unimportance'*. What absurd trivialities they would all seem to future generations, Wells wrote. *'Here are Shaw and I nearing the end of our lives and we can do nothing better with each other than this personal bally-ragging. It is ridiculous to be competitive and personally comparative after 65.'* Sweeping on Wells continued—Everywhere men and women were becoming aware of the shape of things to come; many imaginations were already in touch with a future world and soon a whole multitude would become aware. . . . *'Shaw's attack upon me and my own ill-controlled resentment have set me asking uneasily whether now it is not already time for us to go. . . . Yet I feel that I had rather keep on for a little longer, if only to say at the exit to this dreary class-war dogma: After you!'*

There was a grand melancholy in the impatience, a very difficult mood to meet in argument, but Wells did not for one moment imagine that Shaw would fall silent. And back Shaw came again as alive as ever:

'Order gentlemen!' said Shaw. *'Order please. Remember your international manners.'*

Would Mr Wells never see that Russia had half realized his own dream by producing a 'government of the people, for the people, by men and women who cared sufficiently about the condition of the people, to devote themselves to the work for its own sake?' What *had* come over our Dear H.G.? Granted a high privilege, which, of course, he deserved, he trots into the Kremlin and tells Stalin that his head is over-stuffed with some absurd nonsense called class warfare, when it would so much better accommodate the views of Mr Wells, or the P.E.N. Club whereby Clissoldarity will sanctify the world. . . .[1, 2]

Just look at the situation.

Here we were trying to buy off unemployment with the dole, to frighten trouble away with armaments, to ask for a revival of trade by prayer, while Russia was solving all these problems by rational means. In a recent preface, Shaw said, he had shown that Communism produced not a crude dictatorship *'desperately working the guillotine until the executioner goes on strike'* but *'a self dedicated democratic priesthood organizing a democratic church Militant and an Inquisition held together by a common faith, and by vows of poverty and chastity. To put it in Wellsian terms, it produces the Samurai desiderated by Mr Wells. . . .'*[3]

Shaw swept on to repeat that the privilege of an interview with Stalin was an honour of which the most eminent social philosopher might well be proud. According to Shaw, Wells had responded to this privilege by explaining to Mr Stalin that he was a second rate person victimized by something called Class Warfare.

'I ask H.G. whether he is going to leave it like that. It is useless for him to protest in all sincerity that it was not like that, that he never meant it like that, and that I am all the liars and snobs and slanderers he can lay his eloquent pen to. For this paraphrase of mine is precisely what the interview came to. . . . Stalin, though he has shown that he recognizes Wells as a man of genius . . . cannot be expected to know what we all know in England—namely that H.G. is just like Marx in refusing to tolerate the existence of any other pebble on the beach.'[4]

[1] *H. G. Wells*, p. 207. Vincent Brome.
[2] *New Statesmen Pamphlet,* 1934.
[3] Ibid.
[4] Ibid.

Wells replied: '*Mr Shaw asks whether I am going to leave it like that? The answer is that I leave him like that, gesticulating triumphantly though I suspect with secret misgivings. He can have all the glory of saying that I "trotted" into the Kremlin while, by implication, he and Lady Astor, with the utmost grace, strode, swam, stalked, danced, slid, skated, or loped in, and conversed in some superior imperial fashion of which no record survives. He can have it too, that his burlesque of my conversation with Stalin was the real conversation. . .*'[1]

Momentarily it seemed as though another storm had spent itself—but no. Within a few days Wells stumbled on an old article of Shaw's and at once wrote a letter:

'*Sir, though I have no further retort for Mr Shaw, it may be amusing to the reader to quote what Mr Shaw himself has to say to Mr Shaw. At the time of the Zinovieff letter this is how the celebrated guns were banging it in the* Daily Herald: *Shaw wrote:* "From the point of view of English Socialists the members of the Third International do not even know the beginnings of their business as Socialists; and the proposition that the world should take its orders from a handful of Russian novices, who seem to have gained their knowledge of modern Socialism by sitting over the drawing-room stove and reading the pamphlets of the Liberal Revolutionists of 1848–70, makes even Lord Curzon and Mr Winston Churchill seem extreme modernists in comparison." '

The article went on to say that unless Moscow learnt to laugh at the Third International and realized that the living force of Socialism had left Karl Marx '*as far behind as modern science has left Moses*', terrible misunderstandings would remain. A handful of Russian cranks would solemnly continue to communicate with their counterpart in England, both convinced '*that they are the Proletariat and the Revolution and the Future and the International and God knows what else. . . .*'

To Wells' unconcealed delight worse followed: '*The Russian writings which make the most favourable impression . . . are those of Mr Trotsky, but even he has allowed himself to speak of Mr H. G.*

[1] *New Statesman Pamphlet*, 1934.

Wells with a contempt which shows that he has not read Mr Wells' Outline of History, and has therefore no suspicion of what an enormous advance on Das Kapital that work represents.'

At those moments when he seemed overwhelmed, his own weapons struck from his hand, Shaw became most vital. He at once wrote this letter:

'It was very good of my friend H.G. to reprint that old article of mine; for though it has nothing on earth to do with the present discussion, it proves beyond all question that I have neither a pro-Russian nor an anti-Wells complex.

'Stalin would be the last man on earth to deny that he and his Bolshevist colleagues made an unholy mess of their business at first by trying "workers' control" in industry, and ignoring "the inevitability of gradualism," by suppressing private trade and kulakism before they were ready to replace it; in short that had they begun where Sidney and Beatrice Webb left off, instead of where Marx left off, they would have avoided the crash that led to the N.E.P. and saved some years that were worse than wasted.'

What the Webbs had not taught them they had learnt from bitter experience, and since they knew how to take account of their mistakes. . . . 'The next big book of the Passfield sages will show what Russian practice has to teach us instead of what English theory has to teach Russia. . . .'

There was much more in similar vein until Shaw reached this P.S.:

'I cannot withdraw the word "trotted" as descriptive of Wells' entry into the Kremlin. A man's mood is always reflected in his locomotion. Wells did not strut: that would have been vulgar; and Wells is not vulgar. He did not stalk nor prance in the Shavian manner. He did not merely walk; he is too important for that. Having eliminated all possible alternatives I conclude that he trotted. If not what did he do?'

A pause ensued. Respectively sixty-eight and seventy-eight it was to be expected that their exchanges might lose something of the fire and wit already sustained beyond their natural span, but age proved no restraint on explosions which, if they dwindled away in number, lost nothing in power. Indeed it was some measure of the nature of the two men that within the span of their quarrels they simultaneously fought and brilliantly survived any number of other engagements. Kings of the circle which involved G. K. Chesterton, Hilaire Belloc, Dr Coulton, Henry James, Henry Arthur Jones and others, every one of this array was individually, and sometimes together, locked in 'mortal combat' with Shaw and Wells.

Having a deceptive surface glitter the battles involved principles which passionately aroused all thinking people in their day and age and in part privately, in part publicly, they fought and re-fought issues—political, dramatic, ethical, religious. Far more than echoes come out of these struggles. What they battled over has achieved some resolution today, but the major issues remain as alive and stimulating now as they were then. The clash between Capitalism, Marxism and Socialism is now a vivid reality; the Lysenkoists and Neo-Darwinians are the natural descendants of Shaw's and Wells' biological argument; the attempts to reconcile religion with the growth of scientific humanism, in part the result of Shaw's and Wells' thought; new conventions in the theatre the consequence of Shaw's challenge to Henry Arthur Jones; the disappearance of aestheticism the logical development of Wells' attack on Henry James. So many other issues stem from these two remarkable men. Since it involved both, their quarrel with Henry Arthur Jones demands examination before the Wells-Shaw 'struggle' is carried to its close.

CHAPTER TWO

Shaw and Wells versus Henry Arthur Jones

A T HIS BEST Henry Arthur Jones was a powerful writer whose pen dashed exhilarating prose to paper in the face of fading repute, ill health and an appalling sense that the world was slipping from his grasp. At worst he wasted his talents on defence of dead institutions and imagined grievances. The power of his language matched the weakness of his logic. He would release verbal convulsions of the most remarkable kind but when the rush and noise was over too often the sense seemed oddly thin. As a playwright he was brilliantly successful; as a thinker, inadequate.

Physically there were many resemblances to Wells. Short, slightly built, his energy was boundless, and until the last three years of his life he always took the stairs two or three at a time. Described as noble, his forehead was framed in reddish hair, thick and curly, and his hands were short with square-tipped fingers. To the unconcealed delight of Wells he would tick off points one by one on fingers and thumb, or push back his hat and run his hand over his whole face when a particularly awkward question threatened to embarrass him. Like Wells, words poured away from him, sentences ran together and sometimes foundered in the flood. Mimicry came naturally to both and there were times when they vied with one another to represent Gladstone, Darwin, the Archbishop, Mrs Grundy or—a challenge from Wells which Jones never accepted—God.

Parallels abound in the early days of Wells and Jones, but superficial resemblances produced quite different reactions. Jones went to Mr John Grace's Commercial Academy as Wells went to Mr Morley's College, but Jones left school for ever at the age of twelve, while Wells went on to the Royal College of Science, struggling through a degree. Both suffered in their childhood, Jones concentrating half a dozen hardships which completely failed to warp his mind in the understood manner. He rose at 5, reached the town school at 6, studied until 7, returned home for breakfast, and went into the streets at 8 with a large milk can, selling his father's milk at a penny a pint. By a quarter to 9 he was back at school. A midday dinner was followed by more school from 1.45–4 p.m. and then came milk selling again until evening school at 6. The process of earning while he learnt seemed to delight the energetic young Jones. Later in life he spoke with pleasure of wonderful cream teas, and had no malice towards any childhood memory—except one.[1]

At twelve, Henry Arthur Jones began earning his living, like Wells, in a draper's shop. His daughter, in her biography of him, wrote: '*Henry Arthur loathed and hated the work and loathed and hated his uncle. I do not think he minded very much working fourteen hours a day, seventeen on Saturdays, for a salary of £20 a year, but he could not bear the drab monotony of his life. He longed to get away from it.*'[2]

Wells' own predicament could not have been put more lucidly, although, later in life, he much more vividly evoked the horrors of those wrappered blocks, wooden effigies and tight little men in black, shouting 'Idiot—the silk—show the lady the silk!'

Totally different men emerged from these so similar beginnings. Jones continually regarded the world over his shoulder with a reverence for that past which excited Wells' most crushing scorn. Sixteen years difference in their age left Jones immutably part of the timeless British scene, where right must prevail, the old gods of Gladstone, Dickens and Darwin were still very much in the ascendent, women were solid from the waist down, sex was an unfortunate preliminary to reproduction, and hard work, Sunday observance, and reverence for the Empire

[1] *Life and Letters of Henry Arthur Jones,* p. 29. Doris Arthur Jones.
[2] Ibid., p. 31.

combined to create a way of life only bettered by a select handful in ancient Athens. Wells, straining towards the future, regarded such precepts as humbug from which the British must
quickly free themselves if they wanted to escape the ridicule of
posterity, a ridicule which in Wells' belief should become—and
in much of his writing did become—wholesale condemnation.

The seeds of the battle between Wells and Jones were there
from the beginning. Each represented a microcosm of the opposing ages to which they were born. Destiny demanded that
they should be torn apart, rending each other with increasing
ferocity, although Wells quickly withdrew to Olympian heights
from which he occasionally released a wickedly frank thunder-
bolt calculated to set the words spurting even more freely from
the irrepressible Jones.

Jones, as everyone knows, became a playwright; Wells, a
writer capable of formidable metamorphosis who believed that
he could adopt, with steadily diminishing difficulty, the role of
novelist, scientist, philosopher, world maker, prophet as the
moment required, pouring into each incarnation enough energy
to overwhelm it in preparation for whatever role next took his
fancy.

Jones remained a playwright from first to last with very
great success. At the height of his powers his plays drew large
audiences, brought him wealth and fame, and adequately represented problems of the day with a degree of daring nicely calculated not to shock too far. Immutably correct in his own behaviour he would have died for the code Victoria, going to his
death in the clothing appropriate to the time of day.

For a while, the ascending stars of H. G. Wells and Bernard
Shaw did not overwhelm Henry Arthur Jones, and if his relations with Wells were of a highly ambiguous kind, Shaw regarded him warmly, praised his plays, and always hoped that
the reactionary demons in H. A. Jones would not run amok.

Part of that remarkable milieu which developed at Wells'
House, Easton Glebe, near Dunmow, in Essex, Jones believed

himself *persona grata* in the beginning, and with some evidence. He wrote on December 9, 1912 ' . . . *called at H. G. Wells . . . about 9.45—he had few people there—Rothenstein the artist, Marillier (Mr Fells) partners in Morris'—and a few others. We dressed up in curtains and draperies and danced and played the fool till midnight. I wish you could have looked in. I was draped in a green velvet curtain, with a poker in one hand and a toasting fork in the other, conducting vigorously with both over Wells' head as he played the pianola. Wells was also draped and all the others in anything we could find. We played the fool to our hearts' content.*'[1]

Temperamentally, Jones had far more in common with Wells than Shaw, sharing Wells' delight in games and charades, loving to bound with sheer joy of living. Nothing could be more remote from Henry Arthur Jones' rush of words than Shaw's cut-glass logic; nothing so alien to Shaw as the warmly emotional mists in which Jones exercised his not inconsiderable gifts.

Jones first met Shaw at a meeting of the Shelley Society in the Botanical Theatre, University College, Gower Street, London, in 1885. As the official speeches came to an end, members of the audience were invited to contribute and up shot a lank figure in grey flannels with a flaming red beard. '*Ladies and Gentlemen, I am an atheist, a vegetarian and a Socialist—*' the figure began in a resonant Irish voice. Henry Arthur Jones nudged his neighbour. '*Three damned good reasons why he ought to be chucked out,*' he said.

This unpromising beginning was quickly overwhelmed by a friendly understanding between the two men and presently they were corresponding. Extraordinarily, in no time, Shaw was asking Jones' advice on a highly personal issue. On May 20, 1898, he wrote to Jones:

'*One thing I forgot to say yesterday in writing about Grace Mary [Jones's play]. Have you read Tolstoy's* What is Art? *It is beyond all comparison the best treatise on art, that has been done by a literary man (I bar Wagner) in these times. . . . Among other things he is very*

[1] *Life and Letters of Henry Arthur Jones,* p. 309. Doris Arthur Jones.

43

strong on the Universality of good art, and the classiness of bad—that good art is as intelligible to a peasant as to a gentleman. . . . If there were any chance of his being able to wrestle with the Cornish lingo, I should send him Grace Mary as a striking specimen of the universal play.

'Miss Townsend is quite fascinated by it.

'By the way, would you advise me to get married?

Yours ever,

G. Bernard Shaw.'

Jones replied on May 24, 1898:

'My dear G.B.S.,

'Yes, I would get married if I were you. But read the chapters in Rabelais and the advice that was given to Panurge on the subject. I hope you are getting on all right. I shall look in the first chance I get.

Always yours, H.A.J.'

A few weeks later Henry Arthur Jones received this postcard from George Bernard Shaw:

25 June, 1898

'We are having such a honeymoon of it. A couple of days ago I fell downstairs and broke my left arm; so here I am disabled hand and foot, helpless as a baby. I am only able to scrawl postcards. The lady I talked to so much at the Lyceum—the one on my left—was Mrs Perugini, the one on my right is now Mrs Shaw, with her nice new husband all broken and damaged.

G. B. S.'

When Henry Arthur Jones' play, The Prince's Nose, received cold notices from the critics in March, 1902, Shaw at once wrote to him:

'Dear H.A.J. If there is an occasion on which I loathe a theatre more than ever it is on a first night. And when the business on hand is to murder one of your plays I feel that my attendance is about as friendly an act as a seat in the front row at your execution. If you love me send me a copy of the book; and then when I have had my first impression from you I will slip in some night with my wife and see what they are doing with it.'

Shaw duly read the play and warned Jones a month later: '*You will lose your public if you do not reform at once. Fast, pray, forswear meat and alcohol, turn your back forever on Monte Carlo or you are lost. . . .*'

It is necessary to remember that Jones himself misunderstood the nature of Shaw's plays believing that a beginning, middle and end, suitably interwoven with plot and dialogue were the indispensable requisites of any serious playwright. On November 13, 1913, Jones was writing to Shaw:

'*I have a young friend—who hails your recent enlargement of the bounds of morality. He had written a play which seems likely to advance your views—if we can only get it produced. Its dramatis personae are five Hottentots, eleven monkeys and thirteen goats. There is no coherent story, no vestige of plot and no discoverable purpose. The characters simply come on and talk, talk, talk, talk. . . .*'

Obviously, Jones went on, Shaw was the man to see it through. He might object that the play stole his thunder but if he hoped to continue shocking people he must be '*content with some measure of temporary self-effacement*'.

The turning point in Jones' relations with Shaw and Wells came with the 1914 war. There were to be many strange shifts and alliances between the trio over the next few years but now, ironically, Jones found himself alongside Wells in an attack upon Shaw. To Henry Arthur Jones, nursed in the cradle of the Empire, nourished on imperialism, and the timeless certainty of British justice, Shaw's invitation to the soldiers of the opposing armies to shoot their officers and return home was a piece of intellectual buffoonery not to be tolerated in a situation fraught with the gravest peril for these islands.

Writing from New York to his daughter Doris in 1914 Jones said: '*Shaw continues his crazy attacks. I never felt more angry with any man. He is trying to keep up the strife between England and Ireland. I do not think I can meet him in future.*'[1]

[1] *Life and Letters of Henry Arthur Jones*, p. 310. Doris Jones.

Undoubtedly, Shaw's pamphlet *Common Sense About the War* was a dangerous document, and two of his charges were of a kind which the most emancipated found unforgivable. '*We began it*,' Shaw wrote, '*and if they met us half way, as they certainly did, it is not for us to reproach them.*' Later, discussing the possible consequences of the war, he said: '*If we send the Kaiser to St Helena . . . we must send Sir Edward Grey there too.*'

Open rupture with Jones followed. By 1915 members of the Dramatists' Club could no longer risk contamination by Shaw, and several stayed away from the club rather than jeopardize their reputations. Bluntly revealing this to Shaw the Secretary suggested that perhaps he would prefer not to receive the Club notices, which was, in effect, an invitation to resign. Shaw sent the letter to Henry Arthur Jones and scribbled underneath '*I hope you are not one of the several members, though in these raving mad times it is hard to know. Cheerful sort of Club, isn't it? Ever. G. Bernard Shaw*'.

Jones replied:

'*In reply to yours, I was present at last Wednesday's lunch and I strongly supported the proposal that Paull should write to you in the terms of the letter you enclose. . . .*

'*Your writings on the War have done great harm to our cause in America and neutral countries. . . . Even if what you said was true, it was yet a foolish, mad, and mischievous thing to say at that moment.*'[1]

The letter ended yours faithfully.

Shaw's wit flourished in opposition and within a day he replied to Jones:

' *. . . If you think you are going to put* me *off with a sheet of note-paper containing extracts from the* Daily Express *copied with your own fair hand, you have mistaken your man. . . .*

'*England's cause is righteous. Good; but what is its cause? Besides, it isn't fighting for its own cause, but for Russia's. Are you a sound Russian patriot too? And a true blue Serbian? And do you fill the air with shouts of BANZAI? I take it for granted that you will shed the last drop of your blood for Liberté, Egalité, Fraternité.*'

[1] *Life and Letters of Henry Arthur Jones*, p. 312. Doris Jones.

46

In one sense the letter was vintage Shaw. Intellectual cartwheels had carried him into a contortionist's posture which he alone of living writers could try to justify. Jones threw off restraints. Wit! This was treason not wit. What had praise of the enemy to do with wit when a ruthless war threatened to undermine the very existence of the British Isles and a way of life distilled from generations of pain, struggle and experience.

Imperturbably Shaw protested that his own case against Germany remained intact. Why blame the Germans for claiming him as one of their supporters when the English did exactly the same with any German who rebelled against the brutal idiocies of German propaganda. Why claim that these travesties of his own beliefs, poured out by hack writers, prelates and playwrights who should know better, in any way represented what he had permitted to escape a too fertile pen? *'I had said that to allow the Prussian Military machine to conquer would be to shut the gates of mercy on mankind. The idiot brigade told the world I said it would open them and the Germans said "Hoch the idiot brigade, our best friends".'*

The letter ran on for several pages. The last few sentences began to dance and dive and explode. Not the most grave charges could repress the torrential fountain. *'You [Henry Jones] are like a prize fighter who, with all the points in his favour, has to be shown his unbruised face in a mirror to encourage him to go on. . . .'*

Jones did not reply.

Whatever susceptibilities remained to be shocked were duly outraged when Shaw wrote *August Does His Bit*—a one act skit on war time England, produced by the Stage Society. If his indictment of British war motives was for Jones a reckless piece of misconceived invective, this entered another and far more serious category only to be described as Anti-Christ. Religious fervour came easily to Henry Arthur Jones, and now it generated in him a wrath and eloquence which he could no longer contain.

First he welcomed with agonized relief the criticism of William Archer when the play appeared . . . *'One listens to it with regret. Serious well-aimed satire may be useful but not mere promiscuous persiflage which makes a comic catchword of "our brave fellows dying in the trenches".'*

Amongst the twists and confusions produced during the third year of a war now threatening starvation, it was not unexpected that the ultimate guardian of correct war time behaviour—the Foreign Office—should astonish everyone by relishing Shaw's play. Privately the Foreign Office had suffered at the hands of too many wartime Augustuses—aristocratic noodles who were proud to muddle through—and to the horror of Henry Arthur Jones some of its members were heard murmuring approval of *Augustus Does His Bit.* Mysterious influences presently brought about a far worse state of affairs. Shaw was sent to the Front in 1917 to write a series of descriptive articles which were to be published simultaneously in New York and London. He went to Arras, the Somme and Vimy Ridge, he roared with laughter at a soldier's production of *O'Flaherty V.C.,* drove himself across the dangerous Square of Ypres, saw some of the horror of war and wrote voluminously.

Near apoplexy in Jones quickly gave way to a quiet determination. Lunching at the Athenaeum one day shortly afterwards, he remarked to George Alexander that when a man became as dangerous to a civilized community as Bernard Shaw, someone should crusade against him, and when, later, in the smoking room, Jones discovered that enthusiasm for destroying Shaw precisely matched reluctance to take any action against him, he became—in effect—a dedicated man. Never content with one indestructible opponent, he now considerably complicated his task by simultaneously challenging H. G. Wells. No multiplication of the image of Goliath could dismay this David.

In 1919 Jones published a book, *Patriotism and Popular Education*, attacking H. G. Wells' political beliefs and by implication Shaw's. Ever upright, Jones could not possibly launch the book without warning Wells. On March 11, 1919, he wrote:

'*My dear Wells,*

'*In my forthcoming book* Patriotism & Popular Education *I have attacked what seems to me to be the most mischievous fallacies in some of your recent articles and letters. You advocate principles and schemes which, so far as they can be put into operation, tend to disintegrate and shatter not only the British Empire but all civilized structure. . . .*'

He would be very sorry Jones continued, if this book damaged their friendship but personally he would always dwell with the kindliest remembrance on '*their long and pleasant associations*', and hoped their friendship would ride so small a storm with ease.

All magnanimity Wells replied:

'*My dear Jones,*

'*I am quite sure that nothing you can say about my opinions is likely to alter the very kindly feelings I bear you. I've no doubt you'll go for me with the utmost spirit and violence and firmness. I think the British Empire in its present form is a sham and a nuisance.*

Yours, H. G. Wells.'

No one could have foreseen what dark tides would be released by such a conventionally correct engagement. Occasionally, at the Reform Club, Wells ran across Jones, but the skirmishes which followed were usually redeemed by wit. True there was a reserve in Wells' attitude towards Jones said to conceal an unknown element, but anyone meeting them together might well have believed that here were two writers whose common interest in letters made one reasonably congenial to the other. Yet by September of 1920 Jones was deeply launched into an attack on Wells with a letter which infuriated H.G.

Not merely the war, but the Russian revolution had driven the world out of the complacent assurance that contemporary cultures were timeless, and Wells had horrified half his readers with an article in the *Daily Mail* sympathetic to the new Russian rulers. Jones wrote:

'*My dear Wells,*

'*In a recent article in a morning journal which, I am sure, must have*

*caused you that intense annoyance which we all feel when we find our-
selves injudicously praised in the newspapers—in that article the inspired writer, after an ascription to you of a sovereign comprehension of
human affairs, and a superhuman sagacity in dealing with them, went
on to declare "Wells today is thinking for half Europe." ... Mr
Archibald Spofforth, who was reading the article aloud to me, put it
down at this point and very ungraciously muttered: "Now we know
why Europe is in such a mess".'*

Jones protested that Mr Spofforth was unusually prejudiced
against Wells but

'*I was ... obliged to admit that your advocacy of Bolshevism as the
way of salvation for mankind, your laudation of its leaders as far-
seeing statesmen, "shining clear", "profoundly wise", immeasurably
more competent to guide the destines of a nation than such "pretentious
bluffers" as Mr Balfour and Lord Robert Cecil,*'

did make Wells a dangerous leader.

He understood that Mr Wells intended to go to Russia to find
out the facts for himself. Why was it necessary? They were already abundantly clear. Clouds of witnesses had returned and
avowed '*the terror that reigns there; all the securities and sanctities
of civilized life abolished; all the spiritual and all material possessions
of the people seized and escheated ... sweated labour, gagged and
fettered against all complaints and strikes ... a ruthless militarism,
more brutal than the German ... a junta of desperadoes coining the
blood of wretched peasants into gold to send to England to blind and
drug our workmen, and to raise them into insurrection against their
own means of livelihood. ...*'[1]

A rush of words to his pen sometimes carried Jones away into
a world of imaginative fury which gave extraordinary life and
vitality to the boldest forms of myth. There might be a great
deal in what he said, but even close friends thought he overdid
the Russian desperadoes a bit.

Wells replied on September 16, 1920:

[1] *My Dear Wells*, pp. 1–5. Henry Arthur Jones.

'*My dear Jones,*

'*Your letter is much too silly to notice in any matter except one. You put "shining clear" and "profoundly wise" in inverted commas as if I had used them for the Bolshevik leaders. This is not the case. It is also a lie to say I have lauded its leaders as far-seeing statesmen and "declared my preference for Russia and Bolshevism" as against England. The rest of your rant seems to be based on this misconception. . . .*'

Some further exchanges followed between them and then Wells wrote:

'*My dear Jones,*

'*Your attempt to justify your charges has obliged me to make a journey to the office of the* Daily Mail *to look up the articles you pretend to quote. As I expected, you have cut out words and phrases with disregard to the context. I will try to imagine there is a sort of honesty in the way you have twisted these clipped extracts against me but I'm afraid that in doing so my impression of the entire silliness of your rodomontade is very much deepened. To make it clear just what you have done I shall be obliged to go over the general substance of the article in question.*

'*The article of January 15, 1918 (note the date) is an attack on our British diplomatic methods and on the probability, which then seemed a considerable one, of a patched up peace with German imperialism. In it I say that having failed the Kerensky Government by not going into the Baltic with our Fleet (cf. Lord Fisher on this topic) and having allowed our monarchist sympathies to weaken the young Russian Republic until it fell to the Bolsheviks, I say (January 15, 1918) we know very little about them. I say they are "probably honest" and straight. Don't you think they are straight? They are trying, as we are trying to revolutionise Central Europe, and so end aggressive militarism in the world forever. They believe they can do this by mental work, by propaganda. I suggest (January 15, 1918) that this is something we might very well learn from them. (Shortly after this I took charge of the German propaganda at Crewe House.) Then I go on to question whether we are wise in treating them as "ignorant, illiterate and inexperienced men of no account".*

'*I point out that like Mr Lloyd George, they are mostly poor men of the professional class. On the other hand they are "better educated"*

. . . than our own diplomatists. I do not "laud them as far-seeing statesmen", that is just a ranting phrase of yours, but I point out that almost all of them know "English and German as well as Russian". I am comparing them with our diplomatists. Our late Ambassador in Petersburg never learnt Russian and our official ignorance outside Court circles in Russia was colossal.

'*I then attacked Mr Philip Snowden and Lord Lansdowne for their attempts to make peace with the Hohenzollerns.* Upon this issue "*No peace with the Hohenzollerns*", the Bolshevik are shining clear. *Would that our people had half their clarity! Obviously* on that point, *I should have thought that no one but an excited imbecile would suppose it meant that they were "shining clear" without that qualification.*

' "*If we seek a mean immediate peace,*" *I say* "*instead of supporting the Bolsheviks in their bold but profoundly wise insistence upon a peace of the peoples, we shall not achieve that reconstruction (the reconstruction of Europe) because the Hohenzollern tradition will prevent it.*"

' "*World wide famine, world wide brigandage, the cessation of education, the ending of trade and traffic; towards these things we step today, if today we treat this cancer of German monarchy and the diplomatic plotting that is inseparable from it as though it were not the supreme evil against which we fight.* In these things, *it seems to me (January 15, 1918) the Bolsheviks are altogether wiser and plainer than our own rulers.*"

' "*In these things.*" All such qualifying and limiting clauses slip past your hasty, ill-trained mind. You want to rant and nothing will prevent you from ranting. Of any preference for Russia to England, there isn't a word in this article or in anything I have ever written.'

Jones replied on September 17, 1920:

'*My dear Wells,*

'*I accept such terms as* "*liar*", "*excited imbecile*", "*silly ranter*", "*hasty, ill-trained mind*" *and the other elegancies of epithet which you apply to me—I accept them most cordially, most gratefully, as evidences of your method of controversy. I will treasure them and pay them the same respect that I pay to your social philosophy.*

'*To come to the facts. You accuse me of twisting and garbling your* statements because I quoted you as saying that the Bolshevist leaders are "shining clear" and "profoundly wise". You don't deny that you did call them "shining clear"; but you explain that this applied only to the one matter of making peace with the Hohenzollerns. It is strange that you should applaud them in this matter, when at the most critical period of the war you were urging us to make peace with undefeated Germany under the Hohenzollerns. You will remember I had to curb your zeal when you advised England to throw herself on the neck of her undefeated enemy. So you say that the Bolshevist leaders were "shining clear" on this point only. In that matter, if indeed they were shining clear, I gladly allow that they were far more "shining clear" than yourself. . . .

'Meantime I repeat with the utmost emphasis that I can employ, that your entire article is one continued laudation of the Bolshevik leaders and their far seeing statesmenship, to the depreciation of our English Statesmen. Will you face that simple issue? It is the only main issue that I raised in my letter. . . .

'Your article in the Daily Mail . . . is easily accessible. You do not adjure it. You defend and even reinforce it. I invite and request the fullest comparison of that article with my letter . . . September 16, 1920. . . .

'After all . . . your depreciation of English Statesmen and diplomatists as "pretentious bluffers" . . . "crudely ignorant persons" guilty of vast general incompetence in managing our national affairs, it seems that your chief indictment against them, the head and front of their offending, is that our Ambassador in St Petersburg did not know Russian. If you will enquire I think that you will find that, with one or two exceptions, no foreign Ambassador in St Petersburg has known Russian. It is not a great matter, except in your estimation. Disraeli did not know French. That did not prevent him being a great diplomatist. . . .

'And now, my dear Wells, I must not detain you any further. You are busy packing up for Russia. Let us have some further speech on all these matters when you come back.

'Your sincere well wisher,

'Henry Arthur Jones.'[1]

[1] My Dear Wells, pp. 7–10. Henry Arthur Jones.

Before he left for Russia Wells sent this curt reply:

'*September* 20

'*Mr Jones puts "liar" and "silly ranter" in inverted commas as if I had used these expressions about him. I have not done so. He seems to be incapable of understanding that inverted commas are used to indicate a quotation. He wants to represent me as hurling these expressions at him, or in his undisciplined excitement he forges these quotations, for that is what putting these words in inverted commas amounts to. No doubt he will now say I have called him "forger" or a "convict". Discussion is impossible with such an antagonist. . . .*'

Wells, as we have seen, was away for some time in Russia and came back a divided man. Immediately, fresh letters from Jones assailed him:

'26 *October*, 1920

'*My dear Wells,*

'. . . *I thought it possible that you might be offered some high advisory post in Russia, which your love of the Bolshevist Government would constrain you to accept. For in that country your international theories are being translated into facts, and the general condition of affairs seems to call for constant superintendence from yourself. . . .*

'*I notice that you summarize the conditions in Russia in four words: "Hunger, want but order." This seems to imply that if only order is maintained the hunger and the want are matters of secondary importance. What we are concerned to know is—"How much hunger?" "How much want?" and above all: "What kind of order prevails in Russia today?" . . .*

'*You return to England in good time. Will you tell workers of England—those workers, many of whom were two years ago in the trenches, ready to die for you and for me—will you tell the workers of England that the order now maintained in Petrograd is the kind of order that you desire them to live under? An enforced twelve-hour day, on wages at starvation level; the right to strike, nay the right to murmur or complain denied them under pain of death; free speech more cruelly suppressed and punished than under the worst tyranny the earth has known—will you tell the workers of England that this is the kind of order you wish them to establish in our own country? . . .*

'*When you left for Russia we were engaged in a controversy which*

54

you abruptly closed on the plea that I did not understand the use of in-
verted commas, and that therefore it was impossible to argue with me. I
am quite willing to submit the matter of inverted commas to any impar-
tial judge of inverted commas. But I was under the impression that we
were arguing about those great first principles of civilized government
upon which the security and prosperity of all nations depend.

'*I am anxious to resume the controversy with you on these more im-*
portant matters. Let it not distress you that you find it impossible to
argue with me. I will continue the controversy all alone, and will furn-
ish the necessary arguments for us both.

'*Au revoir,*

'*Henry Arthur Jones.*'

If Wells could be said to break the ensuing silence it was only
in the form of articles appearing in the *New York Times* describing the conflict of hope and depression, carnage and inspiration,
death and resurrection which he found stirring in the great
cities of devastated Russia. They were very frank articles. They
criticized and complained, they drew a vivid picture of Russia
on the verge of anarchy but they were sympathetic towards the
struggle of its new leaders. Jones himself sailed for New York in
November and there continued what for him had now grown
to the proportions of a feud. Letters went personally to Wells—
'*a special thud in the mornings always represented another bomb from
Jones*'—to the *New York Times* and the *Morning Post*. On November 26 he wrote:

'*26 November, 1920*

'*My dear Wells,*

'*I trust you will acquit me of any intentional discourtesy in delaying
replying to your second article on "Russia in the Shadows"* (New
York Sunday Times, *November 14, 1920). It did not reach me until
I arrived in New York a few days ago. I take my earliest leisure to
offer you such comments and criticism as it seems to demand and I ask
your permission to lay them first before American readers and thinkers.*

' "*When a social order based on private property,*" *you say and I
arrest you on these words. You write as if the abolition of private property had been an occasional normal and natural event in history. . . .*

'*Do you not conduct your own affairs with confidence that the British Government (which you lose no chance of abusing) will assure you the peaceful possession of your own motor car and the due payment of your dividends, so that you are thus enabled to "think for half Europe", and so that being yourself a possessor of private property you can safely rail against private property, and being yourself a capitalist you can safely rail against capitalism? . . .*

'*By your condemnation of Marxism principles you bring a deadly unanswerable charge against the present Bolshevik Government. On the other hand, since its first assumption of power, you have praised the Bolshevist leaders as "far seeing statesmen", "shining clear", "profoundly wise". . . .*

'*These and many other laudatory epithets you have showered upon the men who have brought the Russian people to their present dreadful condition, and who, as you carefully explain to us, are now governing Russia on entirely false and vicious Marxian principles. If the body of your disciples in Europe, America, the millions whom you are "thinking for", were able to compare and examine your confused attendances, wouldn't you be in a very awkward position as a leader of European thought?*

'*H. A. Jones.*'

Wells now issued what read like a final edict:

'*December 28, 1920*

'*Being written at by H. A. Jones is like living near some sea channel with a foghorn. You never know when the damned thing won't be hooting again. . . .*

'*Mr Jones trades on the careless hospitalities of my younger days to address me as "My dear Wells" but his heart seems full of malice. Some heedless admirer, it seems, wrote of me somewhere that I think for half Europe. Poor Jones will never forgive me that preposterous chunk of praise. It crops up every time, he cannot get away from it. With that incurable grudge mingles a certain vanity. The ghost of "Jimmy Whistler" haunts these aged gambollings: one feels that at moments Mr Jones really succeeds in feeling that he is being light and witty—"the jester's bauble". It hampers Mr Jones but little that he has evidently never read—more than a few newspaper articles by me. . . .*

'*The jester can always invent a quotation. It is his waggish privi-*

*lege. He says I called Lenin "the beloved Lenin": a lie, out and out,
but who is going to trouble about that? ...*

'*I suppose it's ridiculous to be annoyed by this everlasting hooting
and lying of Mr Jones but I will confess I do find it very annoying. In
the past I have treated Mr Jones in a decent and friendly manner and
somehow that makes this nuisance much more disagreeable. One asks
... what have I done to incur this dreary hostility?*

'*But by this time even your readers must be getting rather bored; he
must have made the point that I think for half Europe at least ten
times; he must have repeated his lie that I called the Bolshevists "shining clear" about a dozen times; he must have said that I am the enemy
of no country but my own two or three score times; and he must have
called me "my dear Wells" several hundred times. ...*

'*As he has nothing else to say whatever I want to suggest to him that
he should now consider the great task of demolishing me at an end, and
that he should turn his wit and eloquence in some other direction. He
shall have all the honours of that sort of controversy. I will confess myself quite overcome by him! Nobody has ever bored me as Mr H. A.
Jones has bored me in the last six months.*'

In reply, on December 30, Jones wrote a tremendous letter
rolling over 21 pages, echoing and re-echoing arguments which
had become familiar to Wells.

On January 6, 1921, Wells wrote to the *New York Times*:

'*... Nor will I argue with Mr H. A. Jones. I never argue with
Mr H. A. Jones. ... I think it is due however to your readers and myself to note that there has been a discussion of these Russian papers of
mine in the English press. It occurred in our sluggish, old world fashion
after the publication of the last article. Our Mr Winston Churchill
made a brilliant attack on my point of view and this gave me an opportunity of discussing the more violent types of anti-Bolshevist mental-
ity.*'

Far more abusive phrases crept into another letter which
Wells now wrote. Referring to Jones he said: '*One might as soon
expect reason from three pennyworth of catsmeat as from a mind of this
sort.*' And later: '*This poor muddled and I fear afflicted mind is challenging me.*'

Untroubled Jones wrote on January 23:

'*My dear Wells,*

'*The wise men of Laputa, as Gulliver tells us, were so absorbed in their own ideas, and so wrapt away from the obvious fact under their nose, that they needed a constant attendant to recall them to the actualities of life so that they might not damage themselves by knocking their heads against any post or by falling over any precipice that was in their way. These attendants carried a blown bladder, fastened like a flail at the end of a stick and filled with dry peas or little pebbles. They were called "flappers", a name which is now used to denote a much less useful class of persons. Whenever it was necessary to waken a Laputian philosopher to some obstacle in his path, or get him to abandon his vagaries and listen to serious discourse, his flapper would give him a slap on the face with the bladder.*

'*Being impressed with your striking resemblance to the Laputan Philosophers I resolved that I would put aside less urgent business and constitute myself your flapper, in the Laputan sense.*'

Before following Jones in his new found profession, Wells' battle with Churchill needs some examination. Nothing if not intellectually tough Wells—who delighted to grapple with half a dozen giants at once—had pitched into Churchill in his customary manner. The shop assistant raised to a tenth power never failed to cock a magnificent snook and while he continued to receive Jones' letters with one hand, with the other he dealt with, or tried to deal with, Churchill.

Clearly, when Churchill challenged him he knew the mettle of his opponent but perhaps underestimated his power to speak his mind in public. According to Churchill's biographer, Lewis Broad, he was, in the early 1920s, fresh from his successes in demobilization at the War Office, a mere stripling of 47, with all the ambition and arrogance which the line of Marlborough and a tremendous array of talents could generate. T. E. Lawrence had set his seal on Churchill's work in the Middle East as Secretary for the Colonies, and if British soldiers were fighting on Russian soil, their numbers were negligible, policies confused, and Churchill's sturdy hatred of some barbarism symbolized in the word 'Reds', shared by a great part of his fellows. Wells' comments on Russia may have shocked Jones; they inspired Churchill. He wrote:

'When one has written a history of the world from nebula to the third International and of the human race from protoplasm to Lord Birkenhead in about a twelve month, there ought to be no difficulty in becoming an expert on the internal conditions of Russia after a visit of fourteen days. When a writer of such singular power and imagination as Mr Wells turns aside from those charming philosophical romances with which he has so often delighted us, to give us definite and final guidance on the greatest political question in the world, we ought to examine his conclusions with attention.'[1]

Churchill proceeded to summarize Wells' articles in the *New York Times* under three headings. First, according to Churchill, Wells said that nothing like this had ever happened to Russian civilization before; it was in extremis and would collapse if the existing chaos continued for another year. Second, the Bolsheviks were the only possible government capable of staving off disaster. And third, the inexperienced Bolsheviks should receive generous help to establish a milder communist order.

Rolling away in what Wells regarded as rhetoric, Churchill continued: ' *. . . In order to separate truth from error in these propositions, it is necessary to begin the argument at an earlier stage. The scientific apparatus which has rendered possible the great expansion of the populations of the world in modern times is the result of capitalist production by individual effort. And from much earlier times the power of men to form themselves into civilized communities depended upon the observance of laws which secured personal possession of the fruits of work, enterprise or thrift, which procured respect for contracts entered into.'*

'The world at last in the nineteenth century had got rid of slavery and had liberated in every land the native energies of man. The demand of the French revolutionaries, "la carrière ouverte aux talents",

[1] *Daily Express,* December 1920.

had been fully met. In Britain, on their merits, without any revolution, a private soldier became Chief of the Imperial General Staff and a lad from a Welsh village became Prime Minister.'

The rhythm deepened as the paragraphs developed. '*The Christian revelation and other revelations suited to other skies and climates all sought to extend the human vision beyond the limits of this transitory world . . . to afford consolation in sorrows which no human laws can assuage. This path also was open and free for all who wished to follow it.'*

These ideas, Churchill said, were repulsive to a sect of men living in the underworld of our great cities. They pursued the principle of absolute equality which produced a world of equally hungry slaves instead of unequally prosperous freedmen. . . . '*The miseries as yet unrelieved and the wrongs as yet unredressed of large classes of the population, particularly in great cities, lent a driving power to their doctrines.'*

They were men given to murdering distinguished citizens as a token of their faith, they would brutalize and suppress, they were the men who had risen in Russia ' . . . *and now Mr Wells that philosophical romancer comes forward with the proposition that* [*this*] *cancer is the only thing that can pull the body round.'*[1]

From Wells' point of view, sheer oratory had carried Churchill into a world of images where cancer, wealth, disease and human physiology had replaced the true facts to their confusion.

His answer on December 11, 1920,[2] began innocuously enough: '*When I first read our Mr Churchill's "reply" to my description of the things I saw and the personalities I met in Soviet Russia, I was inclined to leave him unanswered. Reply there was none. My poor observations were ignored. Mr Churchill has not even noted that I do not ascribe the present condition of Russia to the blockade.'*

Slowly the old Wells broke through: ' . . . *Although I am an older man than Mr Churchill and have spent most of my life watching and thinking about a world in which he has been rushing vehemently*

[1] *Daily Express*, December 1920.
[2] *Daily Express*.

60

from one excitement to another, he has the impudence to twit me with superficiality. He makes the cheap debating point against me that I have written an outline of the world's history as though that convicted me of presumption. . . .

'*He believes quite naïvely that he belongs to a . . . gifted and privileged class of beings to whom the lives and affairs of common men are given over, the raw material of brilliant careers. . . .*

'*It seems to him an act of insolence that a common man like myself should form judgments upon matters of statecraft. . . .*'

Thus, said Wells, he disposes of me. '*But Mr Churchill not only poses as a statesman; he is accepted as such. He is the running sore of waste in our Government. . . . He has smeared his vision with human blood and we are implicated in the things he abets. . . .*'

Wells was in full stride at last. Quickly, acidly, he sketched what he regarded as the results of the 'philosophy' for which Churchill stood. Beyond the earthly rewards of private enterprise, the far less dubious rewards of a hereafter enabled those bereft of satisfactions in this life to live eternally on the verge of achieving them in the next.

He continued: '*Mr Churchill is an adventurer. . . . His imagination is obsessed by dreams of exploits and a career. It is an imagination closely akin to the d'Annunzio type. He is a great student and collector of the literature of Napoleon, that master adventurer. Before all things he desires a dramatic world with villains—and one hero.*'

Wells himself did not believe that this small movement in Russia would ever come to dominate the world, but it was imperative that men like Churchill should be forced to recognize their place in the New Order. It was no use his falling into grand postures, for a world no longer impressed by such antics. '*What a spectacle of utter bankruptcy moral and intellectual he presents,*' Wells added. No one, it seemed, could withdraw from terms as concrete as that, and if, a moment later, Wells was saying '*I cannot call myself anti-Churchill—I have known Mr Churchill for a dozen years perhaps and there is much to like in him*', magnanimity was short lived.

This immediately followed: '*I will confess that it distresses me that he should hold any public office at the present time. These are years of great scarcity and Mr Churchill is temperamentally a waster; there are dangerous corners ahead and for years Mr Churchill has—if I may use the most expressive word—monkeyed with our Eastern policy. . . . I want to see him out of any position of public responsibility whatever. . . . His presence in the Government taints his colleagues and the Prime Minister with a flavour of cynicism. . . .*

'*The Government would look more serious and statesmanlike without him. And the retirement of Mr Churchill would not be a tragic fall such as Lord Haldane's for example. Mr Churchill has many resources. He would, for instance, be a brilliant painter. . . .*'

Only those who knew how scathing Wells could be about '*a bloody painter*' savoured the full irony of this last remark. None of it passed unnoticed by Henry Arthur Jones. The last ten years of his life were seriously damaged—in the dramatic sense—by his fixation on destroying the beliefs of H. G. Wells, and intermittently, Bernard Shaw, and he regarded the intervention of a man so distinguished in public affairs as Churchill, as heaven sent.

February 25, 1921, brought another huge letter from him to Wells which began:

'*The more I study this reply of yours to Mr Churchill, the more I am fascinated and absorbed by it. It is so nebulous in phrase, so opulent in fallacy, so triumphant in assumption, so brazen in self contradiction, so cocksure in wild unproved assertion. . . .*

'*From a score of kindred passages I pick the following: "But does Mr Churchill really believe that the men who created all this vision of hope . . . the patient men of science, the inventors and writers and teachers, did it all for private gain, or for the aggrandisement of a family?"*'

Jones commented: '*Some of them succeeded in getting much private gain, and in founding families; some of them did not. Probably most of them worked as most of us work, from the honourable motives of getting private gain, and also of getting fame and influence. Shake-*

speare made a comfortable fortune out of popular play-writing. As Goethe says "Shakespeare and Moliere wanted above all things to make money out of their theatres".'

Accepting Wells' foghorn definition, Jones proceeded to repeat the appropriate noises in this letter with comic effect.

'You demand of Mr Churchill whether he has the "assurance to tell us that the rich men of today and the powerful men of today are anything but the interceptors of the wealth and influence that quite other men have created for mankind?"
'Do you mean all, or approximately all, the rich men, approximately all the powerful men? If you do, then no more monstrously and transparently false and absurd notion ever entered a man's head. TOOT! TOOT! TOOT! HOOT! HOOT! HOOT! Open your eyes my dear Wells. Let me give you a resounding thwack with my flappers' rod and bladder. POP! Awake! Awake to the facts. . . .'

Irreparably blind to the subtleties of economics, Jones never grasped Wells' point that wealth was far too often in inverse proportion to ability, effort, or talent, and that financial manipulators, in Wells' view, were not the most desirable beings upon whom to lavish immense rewards.

Receiving no answer Jones fired off one letter after another. On March 16 came this:

' . . . In the comparative absence of high comedy from our English stage, I find a satisfactory substitute in contemplating the magisterial attitude you adopt towards Mr Churchill, and the lofty tone of the reproofs you administer to him. In your majestic cocksure philosophic dignity of bearing towards him, you show yourself to be sublime—or at least not more than one step removed from it.
'Nothing in the whole paper pleases me more than your portentous declaration "Mr Churchill has an undisciplined mind." You say so. You talk, my dear Wells! . . . Everybody who opposes you has an undisciplined or a hasty, ill-trained mind. Do you mind my pointing out to you that you do not settle a question that is in dispute by telling your opponent that he has an "undisciplined" or a "hasty ill-trained"

mind? That may seem to you a convenient way of escaping from argument and of course if you find yourself floored, you may as well say that as anything else. Nevertheless it is a bad habit. . . .'

Normally hostile to anything resembling statistics Jones now brought figures into the battle with considerable effect. Wells' attack on Churchill, he said, contained:

17 lines of doubtful argument upon the matters in dispute.
165 lines of detraction and abuse of Mr Churchill.
149 lines of illogical advancement of his own theories.
206 lines of unclassifiable generalities and irrelevances.

Wells received these and a stream of similar letters in blank silence. Nothing could break his determination to ignore Henry Arthur Jones. Its effect on Jones was to redouble the number and turbulence of his words, until at last he wrote what must be the longest sentence in the English language. It was an attack, this time jointly on Shaw and Wells and brought 602 words into loose association without the glimmer of a full stop. Electrically alive, the whole tremendous outpouring ran from one page to the next, revealing remarkable powers of writing, if the device of substituting dashes for full stops was not in the highest tradition of English literature.

'Then you George Bernard Shaw face me and answer me . . . you, whom in the years before the war, this foolish country nourished and caressed and dropped herself bedazzled at your feet, when your brazen wit bullied her to believe that black is white, that square is round, that wrong is right, that two and two make five—you, who when the war came, put on new cap and bells and declared yourself its arbiter; plugged its engines of death with your squibs and crackers, and perked yourself to boss its dreadful issues—you, who in the black resplendent hours of the first Ypres fight, when England was beggared of munitions, furnished her foes with an arsenal of slander and lies—you, who, when we were nerving ourselves for our tremendous task, when every English soldier's heart needed to be steeled that England might be preserved and that you might be preserved to gibe at England—you, who then

64

counselled the brave fellows who were agonizing to save your traitor's skin, to shoot their officers, desert their flag, and thus precipitate such wide ruin and havoc. . . .'

So it ran over three pages; resplendent, echoing sentences piling up into a majestically mistaken letter.

Not only Wells continued silent as the grave; so did Shaw. Jones now conceived the idea of collecting his letters, concentrating his attack in book form, and launching this fresh onslaught on Wells. Whereupon H. G. broke his long silence with a letter to Messrs Dutton, its prospective American publisher, warning them that Jones must get his inverted commas in the right place or trouble might ensue. At once Jones wrote to Wells. August 10, 1921, brought this reply in the *Morning Post* from Wells:

August 10, 1921

'*Mr Henry A. Jones has sent me a cutting from your columns, a two column letter which he has addressed to me and which you have obliged him by printing. Mr Jones professes himself under the impression that I have threatened him with an action for libel. I should as soon think of bringing an action for libel against a barking cur. Some time ago Mr Jones instructed his secretary to inform me that Messrs Dutton were publishing the wild tirades he has been making about me for—I don't know how long—it seems like ages—in book form. As Messrs Dutton & Co are respectable publishers I wrote asking them to see that what Mr Jones pretends to be quotations from my writings, were quotations. This has apparently hung up his precious publication in America. But I have told Messrs Dutton that I do not care a rap what Mr Jones says about me so long as he never tells positive lies, nor implies them by using inverted commas about words or phrases I have not employed. . . .*

'*I ask you what is one to do about a campaign of this sort? One cannot waste time and trouble in litigation and disputes about this man's silly repeated falsehoods. Nevertheless they are a very serious annoyance to me. It is like being persistently shouted after in the streets or having one's doorbell rung at all hours. . . .'*

The following day Jones replied:

'You have certainly given Messrs Dutton the impression that you will bring action against them if they publish My dear Wells, *for they have asked me to guarantee them against the costs. However I gather from your letter . . . that on renewed consideration you have now abandoned whatever intention you had of taking legal proceedings. I also understand that you do not propose to take advantage of my offer to submit the proofs before publication, to some impartial literary judge.'*

Correspondence now concentrated upon a remarkable letter of Wells, written privately to an American author. Wells had said in the letter:

'Don't write me down a Bolshevik. I'm a Wilsonite. . . . For the first time in my life there is a man in the world that I am content to follow. . . .

'Lenin, I can assure you is a little beast, like this [followed a drawing of the little beast]. *He* [Lenin] *just wants power and when he gets it he has no use for it. He doesn't eat well, or live prettily, or get children, or care for beautiful things. . . . Lenin is just a Russian Sidney Webb, a rotten little incessant intriguer. . . . He (Lenin not Sidney Webb) ought to be killed by some moral sanitary authority. . . .'*

Nothing could have delighted Henry Arthur Jones more. He made considerable play with the letter. Was it possible that 'Lenin beloved' as he said Wells had once called him in an effusive moment, had now left him a little in the lurch?

This was too much for Wells; he permitted himself to become involved to the extent of a two page letter written with remarkable restraint:

' . . . This disingenuous and muddle-headed gentleman still clings to the illusion that I will treat his voluminous confused outpourings about Communism, Collectivism, the British Empire, Education and so forth as material for a loud public debate. As I said in a private letter to him which he published, when he inflicted the first discharge upon me, so now, at I suppose the hundredth effusion I repeat that his stuff is too silly for serious attention. . . .

66

'*Thus far for Mr Jones. But his two columns in the* Morning Post *last week contained matter that concerns another person and I will be grateful to you, if you will allow me to make a public amend for that person. I have long carried on a feud, half serious, half humorous, with Mr Sidney Webb. In private discussions, in letters and little caricatures, it has been my habit to guy him and abuse him grotesquely, and among those who understand there has been very little harm done by these freaks. When the Bolshevist revolution occurred in Russia there was a strong tendency on the part of many Socialists here and in America (not by any means Mr Webb) to stampede to Bolshevism. . . . I wrote a letter of remonstrance in the matter to [an American author], which I did not intend him to print, but which promptly got into the papers, in which I spoke of both Mr Lenin and Mr Sidney Webb with how shall I say it—an over-emphatic insistence upon a certain lack of ordinary human sympathy in both of them. Now Mr Jones has dug up this letter. Since it was written I have had an opportunity of seeing and forming and publishing a better estimate of Mr Lenin. But the offence to Mr Webb remains. Will you permit me here to tell Mr Sidney Webb that, this letter and much other girding at him notwithstanding, I have the utmost respect and admiration for the great mass of fine work he and Mrs Webb have done, in social and economic science, and for the lives of sustained and unselfish toil they have lived for the community. . . .*'

Jones' secretary, Hilda Hewett, presently wrote to Wells asking whether he would clarify his precise reactions to the possibility of publication of some of Jones' letters in book form. Wells replied:

'*Dear Madam, I have no objection to Mr Jones publishing any stuff about me that he likes provided he does not tell lies about me. . . .*'

It would be a mistake to imagine that Jones' crusade went unappreciated. Driving at Wells with one hand, he simultaneously launched another book against Shaw—*Bernard Shaw as a Thinker*—and if it was never finished, the first six chapters achieved serial publication in the English Review, and brought this letter from Sir Arthur Keith: '*My dear H.A.J. When you have done with Shaw there will be only feathers and blood left. . . . I enjoy the way you set about him.*'[1] Gwynne, editor of the *Morning Post*, wrote to him '*I like your denunciation of Shaw immensely and although it was certainly personal I think he deserves everything you said of him.*' Later Gwynne said '*Please do not remain under the impression that I dislike the tone which you take over Wells and Shaw. On the contrary, I think you are doing a public service in showing up these two. . . .*'[2] Kipling also sent an equivocal note, and Dr C. A. Alington wrote from Eton College.

When Jones did at last publish some of his attacks on Wells in book form, under the title *My Dear Wells*, Shaw at once reviewed it: '*I am a patient man being naturally timid: but really my old friend Henry Arthur Jones has been a little inconsiderate this time. He has written a book abusing me and H. G. Wells up hill and down dale. . . . But in this book he not only vilipends me with the most amazing copiousness merely to exercise his own powers of invective: he actually finishes by appealing to me in the most moving terms to come and keep up the game with him because Wells will do nothing but call him the most fearful names, and compare his mind to three penn'orth of cats meat. . . .*'[3]

Wells was lucky Shaw said. He had not committed himself, as Shaw had, to Jones' distinction among British playwrights. Moreover Jones and Wells were English which permitted them to pitch into one another without restraint. What was the use of Jones denouncing Wells for *scandalum magnatum* when he spoke scathingly of Parliament, if Jones himself happily referred to it as The Bauble Shop. '*If I take the other tack and hail him as an ultra-incarnadined Red, and try to sing the International with him, he will call the police. Again if I apologize for occasionally chaffing his countrymen for being a little thoughtless he will revile me for being as pitiable a gull as Wells.*'

In an unguarded moment Jones had said—'Show me Socialism in actual operation on no matter how small a scale and I will

[1] *Life and Letters of Henry Arthur Jones*, p. 324. Doris Jones.
[2] Ibid.
[3] The *Sunday Chronicle*, November 20, 1921.

become a socialist.' Shaw now accepted the challenge. '*I know very well that if I point out to him that London which is not a particularly small community, depends for its very existence and possibility on pure Communism in highways and bridges, scavenging and lighting, police protection, military and naval defence, public health service, the Throne . . . the National Gallery and the British Museum Library, the parks and open spaces, not to mention the Collectivism to which we owe our municipal electric light services, our public baths and so forth, he will throw his boots at me and go on telling Wells on every third page that he owes the quiet enjoyment of "his motor car and cosy dividends" not to our Communist police force, but to the private capitalists who are standing heroically between Wells' garage and that notorious motor car snatcher, Lenin. . . .*'[1]

As for Jones' appeal to Shaw to join in the battle: ' "*Take up my challenge which he refuses*" he (Jones) *cries. . . . "You will not pompously and fatuously announce as he does 'I never argue with Henry Arthur Jones' " . . . But what good will jibing at Jones do? On the face of it he has got himself into a mess. If I mount the literary high horse, and stand on the common civility due to Wells as one of the greatest living English writers, I must say with pompous austerity that this book is a shocking book; that it should never have been written. . . .*'[2]

Jones was deeply hurt. Unlike Wells, Shaw had sustained that glorious good humour in his exchanges with Jones which characterized his relations even with enemies. He had befriended Jones. This review seemed to Jones uncalled for. He still could not believe that the justice of his attack on Wells was not painfully evident to any writer, politician or artist with the vaguest pretentions to patriotism.

Friends and family had done their best to prevent him from continuing to use up his declining energies in these attacks; they had become stale and unprofitable, they said;[3] but not even

[1] The *Sunday Chronicle*, November 20, 1921.
[2] Ibid.
[3] *Life and Letters of Henry Arthur Jones*. Doris Jones.

Jones' doctor could dissuade him from a task which he had come to regard as a high mission to which he had been called.

Two years intervened between the publication of *My Dear Wells* and the production of his play *The Lie*, and those two years changed Henry Arthur Jones. The combined force of increasing age, doubt about his powers to satisfy modern audiences, and a dim apprehension that perhaps his battles with Shaw and Wells were mistaken, brought about what was described as a nervous breakdown. This did not interrupt the production of *The Lie* or Jones' appearance in the theatre. His family, afraid that he would publicly belabour Shaw and Wells, implored him not to make a first night speech. Lady Wyndham sent a tactful note saying that he should not '*take a call*'.[1] Undecided, Henry Arthur Jones went to the theatre. Tumultuous applause overwhelmed all precautions and Jones duly made a brief speech while friends waited anxiously for the inevitable references. They did not occur. The curtain fell, police were called to protect him from his admirers, he signed autographs and prepared himself for the critics. Some regarded *The Lie* as a brilliant example of Jones' work, others referred to the play as old fashioned; some plainly did not like the play. Altogether it was a normal enough reception; but great new forces were disrupting dramatic no less than political principles and that resilience which might have reconciled him with the new outlook was not easily achieved at seventy-five.

The Lie undoubtedly succeeded. It ran at the New Theatre for 187 nights. Then, to Jones' horror, it was taken off to make way for Shaw's *St Joan*. The Cassons successfully revived the play eighteen months later, but there was something symbolic in its sudden cessation while still playing to big audiences, and the irony of substituting Shaw could not have been more savage.

The Lie is the story of two sisters, one a devoted unselfish woman, Eleanor, who protects her younger sister Lucy when she has an illegitimate child. Both fall in love with Gerald Foster

[1] *Life and Letters of Henry Arthur Jones*, p. 336. Doris Jones.

and Lucy, when questioned about the child, allows him to think it belongs to Eleanor. The impetus of Jones' dialogue swept away the difficulty that any cross-examination of Eleanor would inevitably reveal the truth and permitted Lucy to marry Gerald with some conviction, while Eleanor's love for the child and the old-world chivalry of Noll Dibdin, Gerald's friend, promise to restore her to some measure of happiness.

Bursting into this very effective Victorian drama with the shock of an intellectual bomb, Shaw's *St Joan* exploded every convention. It outraged dramatic technique, and occasionally achieved a sublimity of language. It could be said that the play began, continued, reached a number of climaxes and subsided into silence, but that exquisite balance of plot and character, that organic unity which Jones had been taught must mark any play with serious pretentions, was not merely absent but deliberately flaunted.

Shaw's growing popularity had baffled Jones, and now, the inexplicable substitution of *St Joan* for *The Lie* left him bewildered. The death of his mother occurred shortly after the production of *The Lie* and struck a fresh and terrible blow. Elements of real tragedy, rather more stark than anything contained in his plays, now gathered force in his life. He was a simple man, easily moved, and his relations with his mother had reconciled a deep devotion with that kind of language which permitted him to signal in deaf and dumb alphabet when she was very ill: '*The best wife a man ever had.*'[1]

He was already ill with flu when she died and presently the combined effects of literary feuds, illness, loneliness and distress at her death, made necessary a nurse. Signs of what he was feeling appeared in the nightly ritual which developed between himself and the nurse when she would say '*have you everything you want for tonight Mr Jones?*' and he replied '*Everything except peace of mind, nanny.*'[2]

---

[1] *Life and Letters of Henry Arthur Jones,* p. 340. Doris Jones.
[2] Ibid., pp. 340–41. Doris Jones.

A splendid four volume edition of Jones' plays edited by his old friend Clayton Hamilton appeared in 1928 to his infinite delight, but by now his dependence on his daughter had reached a pitch which she found distressing and no amount of professional success could reconcile the fears and worries which pressed in on him. He could not bear Doris Arthur Jones to be out of his sight. If she had a dinner engagement it was necessary to arrange for a substitute to sit in. She wrote '*the dear old man was so very pathetic in his dependence on me: so unhappy and distressed when there was even a temporary cloud between us*'.[1]

Jones' final attack on Bernard Shaw has never been published. It is contained in a curious little book only six copies of which exist. It was inspired by the combined effect of Shaw's attack upon Shakespeare and what seemed to Jones the monstrous injustice of an invitation to Shaw to propose the health of the poet at the annual festival in 1925. With that extravagance which redeemed the worst excesses of his conceit Shaw had written:

'*With the single exception of Homer there is no eminent writer, not even Sir Walter Scott, whom I can despise so utterly as I despise Shakespeare when I measure my mind against his. The intensity of my impatience with him occasionally reaches such a pitch, that it would positively be a relief to me to dig him up and throw stones at him. . . .*'

Jones simply did not understand talk of this kind. Once more his wrath ran over into ninety-five pages. '*In Nineveh before it threatened destruction there were six score thousand persons who could not discern between their right hand and their left. In England there are a hundred times six score thousand persons who cannot distinguish between the rank sedition that is seeking to destroy this land and the steadfast loyalty that is seeking to save it. . . . Thou hast him there Stratford-on-Avon, this petted hater of England and glorifier of Red Alienism; thou hast him there, hugging him to thee while he displaces and denies Shakespeare. Which of these two wilt thou extrude—Mr Mayor of Shakespeare Town? For neither in Stratford, nor in any*

[1] *Life and Letters of Henry Arthur Jones*, p. 340–41. Doris Arthur Jones.

man's mind that is illumined by clear and ordered thoughts can these twain dwell peaceably together. . . . *Will you not arouse yourself Mr. Mayor to do what you may to purge your town?'*[1]

The Mayor appears to have remained singularly immoved. Shaw duly faced the Stratford whose patron saint he scorned. When Jones attempted to publish this new attack on Shaw, there was a struggle in Nash and Grayson between Eveleigh Nash pressing for publication and the remainder of the directors who were against publication. The majority prevailed. Jones tried several more publishers in Britain and America. Invited to guarantee that he would take no legal action, Shaw refused on the grounds that the sooner Henry Jones stopped wasting his energies in these attacks, the better it would be for British drama. In desperation Jones persuaded a local printer to set up his book, but when the printer heard Shaw's decision, panic overtook him and after six copies had been struck off, he broke up the type.

August 27, 1926, brought this letter from Shaw:

'*My dear H. A. J., I meant to congratulate you on my seventieth birthday but was afraid of sending your temperature up 10 degrees at a critical moment. I am assured now by Max Beerbohm that you are well enough to stand anything; so I insist on affirming that the news of your illness gave me as much concern, and of your safe deliverance as much relief as if we were still the best of friends. Our quarrel has always been a hopelessly one-sided affair; and I have rejoiced in your vigorous invective far too much to feel any malice at the back of it.*'

Shaw sprang on in his muscular prose to explain that some of Jones' ideas were pure Shavian economics, while Jones' article on religion in the *Daily Express* had given him considerable delight.

'*People who obviously pity my dotage have a well meant but disagreeable habit of reminding me that Sophocles wrote his best plays at 80. I suppose they say the same of you. They know nothing about it;*

[1] *Mr Mayor of Shakespeare's Town,* pp. 87–88. H. A. Jones.

but you seem to me to have more drive and style than ever. I wish I could say the same for myself; but at present I feel that my bolt will be shot when I have got through the final struggle and finished my book on Socialism with every word of which you will agree. . . .'

Don't bother to reply Shaw said. The business of birthdays, like recovery from illness, brought a broadside of congratulations through the post office which could easily kill a man outright. There followed this comment: *'Just note that I am not to be shaken off, and turn over for another nap with a groan of resignation. Ever G. B. S.'*

Jones could not bring himself to reply. Any resumption of friendly relations would have seemed to him a betrayal of all those months devoted to his vendetta, and the clearest evidence that the twin demons Shaw and Wells were steadily growing in popularity, made reconciliation impossible. Life was growing more and more difficult for Henry Arthur Jones. Years before he had formed the habit of praying. Once in full daylight his daughter opened his study door to find him on his knees. By October 1928 he was saying to her *'I'm so tired, I'm getting near home Doris, and I don't mind how soon I get there.'*[1] His family did not know that he was suffering from myasthenia gravis, a form of progressive paralysis which gradually undermines all muscular power.

Presently he could not articulate clearly. Signing his name became difficult. He went to see the film production of his play *The Silver King*, but they had to carry him on to the set. January 5, 1929 brought a serious illness, his temperature rose to 103 and acute pneumonia developed. On Monday, January 7, he asked for his cat Ju to be brought to his bed. Replying to some remarks of his daughter Doris, he said: 'I'm so glad'. The words were pitifully indistinct.[2] They were the last they heard him utter.

[1] *Life and Letters of Henry Arthur Jones,* p. 399. Doris Jones.
[2] Ibid., p. 400.

CHAPTER THREE

Henry James versus H. G. Wells

'So THERE, in a manner of speaking, we all were.' That, said H. G. Wells, was a characteristic phrase on the lips of Henry James and one which summed up their long, uneasy, and finally disruptive relationship. It not merely had variations. It was open to such change, counterpoint and allusion that one hour working over the ten words on one occasion produced: *'So that here, not so much locally, though to be sure we're here, but at least temperamentally in a manner of speaking we all are.'*

Less blunt sensibilities than H. G. Wells' might have recoiled from a style so hopelessly overwhelming in these moments. Wells simply said: *'It is leviathan retrieving pebbles. It is a magnificent but painful hippopotamus resolved at any cost, even at the cost of its dignity, upon picking up a pea which has got into the corner of its den. Most things, it insists, are beyond it, but it can, at any rate, modestly, and with an artistic singleness of mind, pick up that pea.'*[1]

One can hear the grumble in the Master's throat checked by the need to know its true nature, see the frown on the fine brow, feel the shifting of position in the beautiful armchair, watch the hand reaching out amongst the four so different walking sticks to select the stout one used for more difficult walks across Romney Marsh when horrible reality had sometimes to be confronted. And Wells' reedy Cockney laugh echoing down the lane at the sight of the ponderous figure slowly conveying itself to a safe place where it could momentarily escape the brashness of this—could it be man of letters?

No two men differed so much in outlook, temperament and manners, and had such wonderful equipment to deal with one another's shortcomings. As we have seen, James and Wells were

[1] *Boon*—Reginald Bliss, with an Ambiguous Introduction by H. G. Wells.

present on that disastrous evening in January 1895, when James' play, *Guy Domville*, was hissed and booed in London, and Wells first saw the presence standing white, bewildered but immensely dignified, on the stage. No one knows whether James saw Wells. If so it was their first glimpse of one another. It seems unlikely.. But the memory remained vividly with Wells. Guy Domville was '*one of those rare, ripe, exquisite Catholic Englishmen of ancient family, conceivable only by an American mind,*' who renounced the woman he loved because his religion was more powerful than his passion. George Alexander, in the part of Guy Domville, had an impossible exit towards the last and Wells never forgot the long lean face mouthing the words 'Be keynd to Her. . . . Be keynd to Her' as he disappeared off stage. Nor did he forget the face of James, his mouth opening and shutting soundlessly. Henry James was then 52 and Wells a mere 29.

Thrown together in the next few years by their common interest in literature, the actual shock of meeting seems, on James' side, to have been sensibly delayed. For his part Wells, still gauche in personal relations, still apt to become facetious at any cost and never quite sure of the words which would put people at ease, did not hesitate to meet anyone who interested him. Already a tremendous figure, lowering darkly in the more sacred places of late nineteenth century English literature, James now lived at Lamb House in Rye and presently Wells and his wife took a cottage nearby and correspondence began.

Wells, it seems, had lately read *The Turn of the Screw* and audaciously launched a few shafts at its author. The letter, unfortunately, is lost, but James' reply (December 9, 1898) remains:

'*My Dear H. G. Wells,*

'*Your so liberal and graceful letter is, to my head, like coals of fire— so repeatedly for all these weeks have I had feebly to suffer frustrations in the matter of trundling over the marsh to ask for your news and wish for your continued amendment. The shortening days, the deepening mud, have been at the bottom of this affair. I never get out of the house till three o'clock when night is quickly at one's heels. . . .*

'*Of course I had, about my young woman, to take a very sharp line. The grotesque business I had to make her picture and the childish psychology I had to make her trace and present, were, for me at least, a very difficult job, in which absolute lucidity and logic, a singleness of effect were imperative. Therefore I had to rule out subjective complications of her own. . . .*'

Wells replied on January 6, 1899:

'*Dear Henry James,*

'*I have continued to think about . . . The Turn of the Screw . . . and latterly with an increasing discomfort. Novel and disagreeable as the conviction is, I think that the other alternative is right. The story is not wrong—I was. My conversion was accompanied by the profound conviction of sin and culminated in the small hours. . . . I've had a profitable time and I shan't make such comments on your work again. It isn't at all a lovely story but I treated it with a singularly vulgar lack of respect, and if you were not a novelist, I should doubt of your forgiveness.*'

This last phrase, Wells later explained. A novelist should be ready to absorb any criticism without offence. Coming from a novelist capable of reacting like an angry wasp it had wonderfully ironic undertones; but James did not then know his Wells. Correspondence continued and one day, probably in 1898, Henry James bicycled over to meet H. G. Wells. More letters followed. James wrote a beautiful letter in November 1899 with 'I am coming' as a refrain subtly interwoven into the rhythms of the sentences.

'*My dear H. G. Wells,*

'*You reduce me to a mere gelatinous grovel. And the worst of it is that you know so well how. . . . I think the reason why I didn't write to thank you for the magnificent romance of three or four months ago was that I simply dreaded a new occasion for still more purple perjury on the subject of coming over to see you! I was—I am—coming. . . . Your spirit is huge, your fascination irresistible, your resources infinite.*

That *is much more to the point. And I AM coming. I heartily hope that if you* have *been incommoded it is already over, and for a corrigible cause. I AM coming. Recall me, please, kindly to Mrs Wells, and believe me (I AM coming) very truly* (and *veraciously*) *yours,*

'Henry James.'

In the end Wells went to James. There is no written record of these early meetings, but they must have been something of a shock to James. Each had seen head and shoulder photographs of the other, each knew the other's power over words, but where the ambassadorial presence of James could easily be visualized, the five-foot-nothing little man with a common accent, huskily hooting voice and torrent of words, must have seemed the strangest materialization from the imaginative world in which James had so far contained his disquieting person.

Wells remembered the house, a perfect Georgian house, and the table in the hall where lay the array of sticks, hats and gloves, each combination devoted to its special purpose. James, surprised by the appearance of Wells, distressed by the voice and accent, and overwhelmed by waves of words, stood for a moment considering the array of sticks, as though he would take refuge in explaining their subtleties. That much we know; but little more. It was some time before Wells discovered that a tweed cap, a stout stick and thick leather gloves went with a walk across the Marsh, a deerstalker, a lesser stick and lighter gloves the Golf Club, a light brown felt hat and a cane, the morning walk down to the harbour, and a gold-headed cane with a grey felt hat, afternoon calling.

So far as I can trace, James had lately shaved off the beard which had given his face such a sacerdotal air, and was now bald, his grey-blue eyes serious, the line of the chin powerful, the mouth wide and mobile. His check trousers, patterned waistcoat, cravat and spats, must have been anathema to the carelessly dressed Wells, and some hint which certainly remained of a canon moving with unction and the utmost gravity through a rather too prolonged service, would have distressed him even more. On his second visit H. G. was shown the room looking out on the beautiful walled garden where James wrote, and after two hours returned to his cottage.

The relationship grew. But James, the incorrigible bachelor, James immersed in his world of half-lights, James busy now on yet another book, had little idea that the year 1900 marked a tremendous watershed in Wells' life. In that year Wells moved from the cottage to Spade House, specially built for them by the architect Voysey, and the scene became turbulent with finished and half finished novels, a litter of short stories, essays and satires. Simultaneously his emotional life reached another explosive impasse destined to resolve itself in the most revolutionary manner. For in the year 1900 Catherine Amy and Herbert George Wells, bound by ties of law and affection, came to an understanding about their temperamental differences which was so completely rational it might have seemed cold blooded. Married to a man rapidly becoming a world figure, endowed with remarkable gifts and promising to become wealthy, she now released him from the bonds of the marriage vow and offered him all those physical freedoms which his passionate nature so much craved. Already his affairs had begun, affairs which carried him into a world where every gradation of those magical moods when nothing could stop the tumult of the blood, overwhelmed him.

Against this background James suddenly sent this note to Mrs Catherine Wells, undated:

'*Dear Mrs Wells*,

'*Mrs Wharton, staying with me briefly, had motored me over to Dover to see—and take—a friend (who had also been with me) off to Paris, and on our way back we just tried you on the chance—hoping yet a little fearing. I rejoice that your kind note gives me occasion to explain that with a more premeditated visit we should have infallibly made sure before hand that you were at home and that you gave us benevolent leave. . . . I will come over to you some day with joy, but I am just now asking you to kindly let it—the happy occasion for me—*

wait a little for further definition—as the summer and all the autumn have left my professional integrity shattered by a series of devastating assaults. I must, before I do anything else new whatever, laboriously piece it together again.

'*Yours and Wells's more than faithfully,*

'*Henry James.*'

At last this visit occurred. There is no record of what James thought of the art-nouveau house in which Wells had, at least, persuaded the architect to substitute the spade motif for the heart. Nor is it known whether Wells tried to prod the waxen image of respectability into joining the games he so much loved, or talked blasphemously of science replacing religion. If some of these things must have occurred they did not stop James from repeating his visits, but it is interesting to find him, in the developing correspondence, continuously apologizing for not having answered earlier as if, unconsciously, he already found something distasteful in this little man, and had to bring himself to the sticking point before he could once more acknowledge his remarkable powers. And sometimes, even when he did acknowledge them. . . .

'*29 January* 1900

'*My dear Wells,*

'*It was very graceful of you to send me your book—I mean the particular masterpiece entitled* The Time Machine—*after I had so ungracefully sought it at your hands. My proper punishment would have been promptly to have to pay for it. . . . I re-write you, much, as I read—which is the highest tribute my damned impertinence can pay an author. . . .*'

Already, the double edge was becoming apparent; '*particular masterpiece*' quickly checked by '*I re-write you, much . . .*' If their first meeting had revealed the personal gulf across which they must eternally regard one another, that ambiguity of praise and blame which later upset Wells was already evident in James' words.

Presently James entered his famous third period. To those

who liked to lose themselves in a forest of subtlety this was equivalent to the late Beethoven period; to those who did not, the Master simply escaped from the increasing pressures of harsh reality in his own life, into mists of sheer imaginative finesse. As the call of genius rang clearly in James' ears, he answered it with prayer, complexity and ever more tortuous insights into the obscure crevices of human nature. As if holding a pen interposed a barrier between his thoughts, he now dictated, completing *The Sacred Fount, The Wings of the Dove* and *The Ambassadors.* It was *The Wings of the Dove* which drove his brother William to impatient re-reading of many pages to see *'what the dickens they could mean'.* William came to visit him in 1899, a troubled William, bothered by the increasing obscurity of his brother's work and a new access of sensitivity which made him shrink from seeing too much of Henry in case *'it might yield him little besides painful shocks'.*

One shock it certainly did inflict. Wells had arrived at Lamb House to collect William James and his daughter, and as he approached the door, he heard voices raised in argument as close to heated as the intricate counterpoint of James' talk permitted. Certainly Henry had lost his calm. Certainly he was *'terribly unnerved'.*[1]

William stood pressing his point with an accent unashamedly American, and it was some little while before Henry conveyed, with the help of William, what had taken place.

Discovering that G. K. Chesterton was staying at an inn, the garden of which adjoined Lamb House, excitement had overcome all those niceties of conduct which made up the well bred hush of his brother's life, and William had gone into the garden, propped the gardener's ladder against the wall, climbed up and stared over in the hope of glimpsing the gargantuan figure.

Presently a strange sound between disgust and incredulity drove him to look down at the foot of the ladder. There was brother Henry, mouthing in utter amazement. How William

[1] *Experiment in Autobiography*, p. 538. H. G. Wells.

descended the ladder, Henry at last found words to express his horror and the gardener was summoned to remove the ladder to a safe place is not recorded; but Wells' arrival coincided with the climax of the scene in which Henry's voice very nearly reached a state of being—raised.

And then *'he appealed to me,'* Wells wrote, *'to me of all people, to adjudicate on what was and what was not permissible behaviour in England. . . .'* Instead: *'To Henry's manifest relief I carried William off and in the road just outside the town we ran against the Chestertons who had been for a drive in Romney Marsh; Chesterton was heated and I think rather swollen by the sunshine; he seemed to overhang his one-horse fly; he descended slowly but firmly; he was moist and steamy but cordial; we chatted in the road for a time and William got his coveted impression.'*[1]

Soon James wrote another letter to Wells dated January 20, 1902:

'My dear Wells,

'Don't, I beseech you, measure the interest I've taken in your brilliant book (that is in the prior of the recent pair of them) and don't measure any other decency or humanity of mine (in relation to anything that is yours) by my late abominable and aggravated silence. You most handsomely sent me Anticipations *when the volume appeared, and I was not able immediately to read it. . . . The right hour came, and I gave myself up—utterly, admirably up—to the charm. . . .'*

Once more apologies were followed by admiration, and admiration, criticism. But slowly, in the letters which followed, admiration overwhelmed criticism and soon the criticism had vanished entirely. That Henry James with his inbred awareness of every nuance should finally be swept from his world of undertones into anything so flagrant as admiration, was not only some measure of Wells' impact on his generation: it revealed two characteristics in James which became deeply part of the complicated pattern of their whole relationship.

[1] *Experiment in Autobiography*, p. 538. H. G. Wells.

Michael Swan's excellent essay in *The Cornhill Magazine*[1] analysed one. Swan examined the theme of Master and disciple which ran through *The Lesson of the Master*, *The Middle Years* and *The Death of the Lion* and found a preoccupation in James with a need for disciples. Certainly disciples were to multiply—Hugh Walpole, Percy Lubbock and Logan Pearsall Smith—but, for the moment, it was difficult to see the squeaking, irrepressible, scientific H. G. Wells in the role of disciple to anyone.

Was there another reason? It is possible. Wells had never failed to convey an exuberant sense of 'life' in his work and the sheer joy and rush of narrative made it seem as though he came to his desk every morning bursting with the anticipation which readers now brought to his books. James spoke of Wells' work being—so alive and kicking. Did he envy this quality as he must have envied Wells' sales? Were there, perhaps, moments when he would have liked to find the same *vitality* in his own books? At all events, as nearly as his nature permitted, he now threw aside restraints and wrote to Wells on November 19, 1905:

'*My dear Wells*,

'... *I found your first munificence here on returning from upwards of eleven months in America.... I recognized even from afar (I had already done so) that the* Utopia *was a book I should desire to read only in the right conditions of coming to it, coming with luxurious freedom of mind, rapt surrender of attention, adequate honours, for it of every sort. So, not bolting it like the morning paper and sundry, many, other vulgarly importunate things, and knowing, moreover, I had already shown you that though I was slow I was safe, and even certain, I "came to it" only a short time since, and surrendered myself to it absolutely. And it was while I was at the bottom of the crystal well that Kipps suddenly appeared, thrusting his honest and inimitable head over the edge and calling down to me, with his note of wondrous truth, that he had business with me above.... Let me tell you, however, simply, that they have left me prostrate with admiration, and that you are for me, more than ever, the most interesting "literary man" of*

[1] Autumn, 1953.

your generation—in fact, the only interesting one. These things do you, to my sense, the highest honour, and I am lost in amazement at the diversity of your genius. As in everything you do . . . it is the quality of your intellect that primarily (in the Utopia) obsesses me and reduces me—to that degree that even the colossal dimensions of your Cheek (pardon the term that I don't in the least invidiously apply) fails to break the spell. . . .

'*And now, coming to Kipps, what am I to say about Kipps, but that I am ready, that I am compelled, utterly to* drivel *about him? He is not so much a masterpiece as a mere born gem—you having, I know not how, taken a header straight down into mysterious depths of observation and knowledge, I know not which and where, and come up again with this rounded pearl of the diver. But of course you know yourself how immitigably the thing is done—it is of such a brilliancy of* true *truth. . . .*'

Of course Wells was flattered. Still not entirely free from pretensions of learning from James, he had once asked to borrow the scenarios which James wrote, before launching into a novel, in order to see how they were done. Now, privately he sometimes spoke of James with scorn; but praise from James still mattered to him.

Several meetings followed at Lamb House, Spade House and the Reform Club. Wells himself gave a description of one. Bustling into the Reform Club one day he had almost collided with the slow-sailing, lethargic figure, its big black hat settling into position, its prow retracted, the stomach breasting the door. The eyes were absent and suddenly Wells was struck with the thought that they were the saddest eyes he had ever seen. Sad, perhaps, not only because writers like Wells commanded an enormous audience, but because life, after all, was a sad business to men with Henry James' sensibilities.

James drew to a hesitating standstill, his mouth opened and shut three times and Wells, exploding with life, hopping from one foot to the other, poured out a torrent of words which ran together in a blur. James turned sideways, extended his hand in the direction of the interior, swept off his hat with the other hand, opened his mouth again and remained wordless. Wells followed the direction of his hand, talking volubly, and it was as though the rush of his words sucked James with him back into the club again. Through the corridors they went, Wells hooting away, drawing James on, struggling, behind him.

At last they were settled in the black leather chairs in the smoking room and Wells' bubbling talk admitted the smallest break. And then—according to Wells—as if all his mouthings had been concentrated into achieving this single sentence, James leant forward courteously and said in a hesitant voice; 'I—er— did not quite catch, what it was you said.'

There were many talks. Those who knew James and Wells did not expect them to be anything but tortured.

Answering a question about the authenticity of Landor's experiences in Tibet, James would say: '*Eliminating—ah—eliminating, ah-h—eliminating nine tenths—nine* tenths (slowly)—*of—of —of* (very fast)—*of what he claims—what he claims* (slowly)— *what he claims* (very slow)—*there is still* (fast)—*there—is still— there is still* (faster)—*enough left* (pause) *enough left* (pause) *to make—to make—to make* (very fast) *a remarkable record* (slow)—*a remarkable record ah—ah—*(slower) *a remarkable record!*'[1]

This reply was not in fact given to Wells, but there were similar sentences which Wells could not avoid hearing. One can imagine him seething along their path, just stopping himself from shattering intervention, and then the high voice falling over itself with words, the crackle of laughter, and the forefinger outstretched: a momentary pause and then James' deep accents struggling to speak again, and the slightly Cockney Wells talking on at breakneck speed if only to stop this stuffed image from strangling himself with another sentence: James' eyes widening at such bad manners, but sticking to his absolute refusal to be hustled, making large and soothing gestures to allay anxiety and practically putting his hand on Wells' shoulder and

[1] *The Legend of the Master,* edited Simon Nowell-Smith, pp. 16–17. Elizabeth Jordan.

saying as Sir Desmond MacCarthy has put it, '*Wait—wait. I know, my dear fellow, you are getting fidgety; but wait—and we shall enjoy together the wild pleasure of discovering what Henry James thinks of this matter. For my part I dare not hurry him!*'[1]

Wells had a constant desire to hurry him. Life was urgent, life was pressing. He would have no truck with this eternity of subtlety. But if he has left a general record of the nature of these conversations, there are no very exact details. '*He liked me and he found my work respectable enough to be greatly distressed about it. I bothered him and he bothered me. We were at cross purposes based . . . on very fundamental differences not only of temperament but training. He had no idea of the possible use of the novel as a help to conduct. His mind had turned away from any such idea. From his point of view there were not so much "novels" as The Novel, and it was a very high and important achievement. . . . He saw us all as Masters or would-be Masters, little Masters and great Masters and he was plainly sorry that "Cher Maitre" was not an English expression. . . .*'[2]

Wells was in the shapeless tradition of Smollett, Sterne and Dickens as a novelist, carrying these writers to new depths of social consciousness. Man was very much part of a community; he had work to do which should be adequately represented as work in fiction. There were grubby businesses, inaesthetic implications.

James could not bear anything to be shapeless; commonplace work was not worth representing and Man to him was The Individual dominating society. '*What a piece of work is man!*' Shakespeare had cried and the philosophic implications of the sacred human being working out a personal salvation within a timeless code of values, became to James inviolable. Wells was more pleased by Pope's: '*The glory, jest and riddle of the world,*' and saw Man as just as important as men, following T. H. Huxley's mechanistic philosophy which gave the Race more signi-

[1] *The Legend of the Master,* edited Simon Nowell-Smith, p. 14. Sir Desmond MacCarthy.

[2] *Experiment in Autobiography,* p. 488. H. G. Wells,

ficance than the individual. He represented this view in some of his novels. James' well-bred hands rose in horror.

In 1910 James' brother William died, and Wells was genuinely moved. He had always regarded William as an influence no less deep in his middle age than T. H. Huxley had been in his youth. He wrote at once to Henry:

'*My dear James,*

'*I've heard of your brother's death with a sense of enormous personal loss. As you know, I've seen very little of him but he's been something big and re-assuring in my background for many years and what I saw of him at Rye and Sandgate gave me a very living affection for him. I can imagine something of what his death must mean to you. I'm filled with impotent concern for you. That all this great edifice of ripened understandings and charities and lucidities should be swept out of the world leaves me baffled and helplessly distressed. . . .*'

James replied:

'*We greatly value, my sister-in-law and I, your beautiful and tender letter about my beloved Brother and our irreparable loss. . . . He did surely shed light to man, and gave of his own great spirit and beautiful genius, with splendid generosity. . . . He had an inexhaustible authority for me, and I feel abandoned and afraid even as a lost child. . . . I shall find myself still living upon him to the end. . . .*'

The raw material of living had broken into the beautiful cocoon in which James lived, not only with the death of his brother but the knowledge, now made certain for the first time, that the great collected edition of his short stories and novels had hardly roused any interest at all. It was an appalling combination. The most deeply cherished child stillborn, and a brother who was so much more than a brother, dead. For some time James hardly spoke, did nothing and lay on the sofa.

Slowly the gap left by his brother's death became less painful, but the neglect of the great collected edition continued. At this juncture, Wells produced that extraordinary rag-bag of fiction *The New Machiavelli*, and it was almost as if it became one of many factors to rouse James from his torpor. *The New Machia-*

velli was fair game for anyone interested in protecting the novel from serious profanation. When it appeared serially in *The English Review* there were attempts to stop the story being published in book form. No less than three publishers decided that it was too dangerous to handle, and remembering the enormous potential of Wells' sales, they must have had the strongest motives. When it did appear, either Wells or the publishers found it necessary to send, with the review copies, an extraordinary document called Select Conversations in which Ralph Straus and Wells talked to one another about the book. If the charges of immorality were absurd, the charges of caricature of living people were not. No one who knew her, could mistake the portrait of Altiora Bailey for a searing representation of Beatrice Webb, but where she recommended all her friends to read the book, Balfour, equally plain behind the mask of Evesham, consulted his lawyers. In the well-bred hush of Henry James' world this was bad enough; something far more painful supervened. As I wrote in my own biography of Wells: '*The Story as such had dominated* Ann Veronica, Mr Polly *and* Tono-Bungay, *and social criticism emerged more from character than by direct comment, but with* The New Machiavelli *whole pages, indeed chapters, broke out of the story to indict the dog-fight of politics which should have been a great constructive process, and Remington was swamped again and again by the force of Wells' own opinions, as though he could no longer contain them in character but must burst into the book himself. It was the first ominous eruption of those magnificent moments of self-assertion which were to disintegrate the novelist in him. It was the first moving moment of retreat, the surrender to the huge alter ego....*' Henry James was fast coming to the same conclusion. He wrote a letter from Cambridge, Massachusetts, on March 3, 1911, the last half of which said:

'... *There is, to my version, no authentic, and no really interesting and no beautiful report of things on the novelist's, the painter's part unless a particular detachment has operated, unless the great stew-pot or crucible of the imagination ... has intervened and played its*

88

part—and this detachment, this chemical transmutation for the aes-thetic, the representational, end is terribly wanting in autobiography brought, as the horrible phrase is, up to date. That's my main "critic-ism" on the N.M.—and on the whole ground there would be a hun-dred things more to say. . . .

Wells was still prepared to listen to the Master and—possibly —learn, but his reply made appalling play with a word which to James was anathema.

'*My Dear James,*

'*I've been putting off answering your letter because I wanted to an-swer it properly and here, at last, comes the meagre apology for a re-sponse to the most illuminating of comments. So far as it is loving chastisement I think I wholly agree and kiss the rod. You put your sense of the turbid confusion, the strain and violence of my work so beauti-fully that almost they seem merits. But Oh! someday when I'm settled . . . if ever, I will do better. I agree about the "first person". The only artistic first person is the onlooker speculative "first person", and God help me this shall be the last of my gushing Hari-Karis. But the guts and guts and guts and guts I've poured out all over the blessed libraries and A. J. [sic] Spender and everybody! I run into all sorts of people festooned with the apparently limitless stuff. . . . No!—it shall be the end of it. I wish you were over here. I rarely go to the Reform without a strange wild hope of seeing you.*'

Wider differences appeared on the publication of *Marriage* in 1912. '*With tact and circumlocution*' Wells wrote, '*James broke it to me, that he found a remarkable deficiency in that story.*'[1] James also wrote to Sir Edmund Gosse: '*We must have more talk* . . . *of Wells' book, with which however I am having extreme difficulty. I am not so much struck by its hardness as with its weakness and loose-ness, the utter going by the board of any real self-respect of composi-tion and of expression. Interesting to me, however, your mention of his civil acceptance of your own reflections on the matter, which I should have liked to see.*'[2]

[1] *Experiment in Autobiography*, p. 489. H. G. Wells.
[2] *Henry James and H. G. Wells,* Michael Swan. The Cornhill, Autumn 1953, p. 53.

Marriage tells the story of Trafford, a young man who reck-lessly flies an aeroplane in the days when aeroplanes were hardly known, and crashes the machine into a croquet party organized by the Pope family. Marjorie Pope, the daughter of the house, helps to nurse the not too seriously damaged Trafford, inevit-ably falls in love with him, and suddenly finds her engagement to a Mr Magnet intolerable. Gloom and conflict descend on the household until, one day, two inexpert donkey-cart drivers collide in a nearby lane and there Miss Pope and Mr Trafford confront one another, disappearing into the abyss of three hours talk. Nothing of what they said is represented in the book. They simply emerge with the knowledge that they love one another.

This, James said, just would not do. Wells had called upon him personally and very quickly, as if maturing against this visit, James plunged into elaborate criticism. All very well to have this audacious machine taking the air when heavier than air machines found it hard enough to traverse the roads without trouble, but why lead the reader, in such detail, to this brink, the heart, the core of the matter—a talk in the lane—and then—blank. It would not do. It simply and without equivocation wasn't playing what all artists must at any cost play—the game. '*Why*,' said James, '*I very much doubt H.G. whether you in fact know what was said in that lane.*' And he was even inclined to suspect the verisimilitude of any couple talking for three hours in the lane at such a juncture; which meant—if dear H.G. would see it in the proper light—that he '*had not thought out the indivi-dualities concerned with sufficient care and thoroughness*', he had not *cared* enough about those people.[1] Worse still, the habit by which Wells' characters addressed not other characters but the reader had grown in this book and it was possible, without straining the ears too much, to detect a very familiar squeaky note in Trafford's voice.

Wells listened with that approximation to patience which

[1] *Experiment in Autobiography*, p. 490. H. G. Wells.

expressed itself in restless pacing up and down. He was tiring of all this preciosity; wearying of The Master, The Novel, The Form and all the other magnificent abstractions before which he was supposed to humble himself. So long as the people in the novel *lived*, what did it all matter? '*Henry James was quite right in saying that I had not thought out these two people to the pitch of saturation and that they did not behave unconsciously and naturally. . . .*' His defence simply was that it did not matter, and if it mattered to hypersensitive refinements of the technique of the novel, for the purposes of this particular book it did 'not matter very much.'

There were other things in *Marriage* which distressed James. Trafford was not so much a character as a 'scientific intelligence' and Marjorie Pope was not a woman developed in all the depth of her 'feminine mystery', but a type. These people were cardboard vehicles for Wells' ideas. There remained the speech which Mr Magnet made, a speech Wells had taken almost word for word from the reported speech of a living person. This attempt to harness reality to fiction was not only in questionable taste, but as ineffectual as James expected any direct transcript from life to be. As for the writing—James' ear was shocked by the complete lack of music in so many scamped passages. Wells retorted . . . of course it was scamped, of course it could have been done much better. '*But that would have taken more time than I could afford. I do not mean by that I could have earned less money and been a more conscientious writer, though that consideration very probably came in, but I mean that I had very many things to say and that if I could say one of them in such a way as to get my point over to the reader I did not worry much about finish. . . .*'

Whereupon James wrote another letter. Much later in life Wells described its style as a '*lovely complication of veracity and disingenuousness*'. He referred to James' '*intricate mind, as persistent and edentate as a pseudopodium . . . still worrying round and about the question raised by that story*'.[1] Edentate was distinctly

[1] *Experiment in Autobiography*, p. 491. H. G. Wells.

rude. Among the lowest forms of placental mammal lie the
edentates. Even taken in its colloquial sense of one who has lost
his teeth, it was distinctly personal. But a gap of 22 years extended between that comment and Wells' receipt of a letter
which included these lines:

'*I have read you as I always read you, and as I read no-one else,
with a complete abdication of all those "principles of criticism", canons
of form, preconceptions of felicity . . . which I roam, which I totter,
through the pages of others. . . . I live with you and in you and (almost cannibal-like) on you . . . on you H.G.W. to the sacrifice of
your Marjories and your Traffords, and whoever may be of their company; not your treatment of them, at all, but, much more, their be-
fooling of you (pass me the merely scientific expression—I mean your
fine high action in view of the red herring of lively interest they trail
for you at their heels) becoming thus of the essence of the spectacle for
me, and nothing in it all "happening" so much as these attestations of
your character and behaviour, these reactions of yours as you more or
less follow them, affect me as vividly happening. I see you "behave"
all along much more than I see them even when they behave (as I'm
not sure they behave most in Marriage), with whatever charged intensity or accomplished effect; so that the ground of the drama is somehow most of all in the adventure for you—* . . .'

Disingenuous? Or was it the tortured sensibilities of James,
struggling with his consideration for Wells' feelings and his
microscopic attempt upon the truth, which led him into this
letter?

Much later in life Wells made no bones about it. Sincerity
and insincerity were hopelessly mixed in the letter, he said. He
was quite prepared to admit all the sins. Scenes merely sketched,
characters crudely drawn, types without depth, but '*I had a
queer feeling that we were both incompatibly right*'. The novel as
described by James no more exhausted the possibilities of the
novel '*than the art of Velazquez exhausts the possibilities of the
painted picture*'. Indeed the analogy—brought up by James—
was dangerous. The exact equivalent to Velazquez '*who painted

straight from dwarfs and kings, would be biography, character drawn straight from life'.

Seen against the intricate thinking of Dr Richards or Dr Leavis all this had a naïve ring. The subtleties of modern criticism were unknown in those days, but if strict academic thinking did not greatly trouble James or Wells, in a curious sense the *reality* of the novel did not escape their simple terms as it sometimes escapes the abstractions of certain modern schools. Critically, Wells derived from Matthew Arnold and his belief that our perceptions in literature were not so very different from our perception of fineness or coarseness in life, was shared by Arnold. James derived from Walter Pater where life, in the final analysis, was only tolerable as aesthetic experience, and Proust the ultimate flower of literature.

Any reconciliation seemed impossible: perhaps they never expected it; perhaps they enjoyed the early exchanges as exchanges. Presently Wells made this crusading pronouncement: *'We (novelists) are going to deal with political questions and religious questions and social questions. We cannot present people unless we have this free hand, this unrestricted field. What is the good of telling stories about people's lives if one may not deal freely with the religious beliefs and organizations that have controlled or failed to control them? What is the good of pretending to write about love, and the loyalties and treacheries and quarrels of men and women, if one must not glance at those varieties of physical temperament and organic quality, those deeply passionate needs and distresses from which half the storms of human life are brewed. . . .'*[1]

Wells was not going to be put off by provincial librarians, or puritanical editors who saw fit to refer to certain people in his writings as '*scuffling stoats and ferrets*'. He loved doing violence to the prevailing literary modes, and over a considerable period indulged himself deeply. He was not content with the Established Novel. It held to exterior reactions without ever daring to penetrate inner consciousness. He was going to enter men's

[1] *The Contemporary Novel*—Paper delivered to Times Book Club, 1912.

minds as never before, and the method he would use would be anathema to James, flaunting in the face of all known techniques, a method he could only call the monologue.

Echoes of these words, delivered to The Times Book Club, reached James' ears in Lamb House. Publicly he said nothing, but tensions were developing. Almost simultaneously Edmund Gosse tried to organize an Academic Committee and invited Wells to join. He refused. Whereupon Gosse wrotes to James who at once wrote to Wells (March 20, 1912):[1]

'*My dear Wells,*

'*. . . Is it not possible for you to re-consider—under a fond and passionate appeal, that irresponsive and unsociable attitude? On hearing of your election I felt a greater pleasure than anything in my connection with that body had yet given me, and if you maintain your refusal I shall continue in pain and privation, to yearn for you. . . . I am moved to try respectfully to contend with you to some good issue on the subject. . . .*

'*. . . Don't think I want to harass or overbear you if I say that if these words still leave you cold, I frankly don't want to let the matter go without seeing[?] you over it. I would come up to Church Row—at any hour I might find you—after 3.30 p.m.—for the purpose. . . .*

'*Henry James.*'

Wells was not to be persuaded. He never joined the Academic Committee. There followed James' two famous articles in *The Times Literary Supplement—The New Novel.*[2] They were open to several interpretations. Was the Master becoming a little uncertain of his authority with all these upstart people like Wells and Bennett achieving sales far beyond his own; was he distressed that such loose craftsmanship received such high praise; or had his skirmishes with Wells at last crystallized his own position and forced him to choose the most august platform from which to pontificate? He opened by saying that it was no para-

[1] Text from *Cornhill Magazine*, Autumn 1953.
[2] 1914.

dox to him that the '*state of the novel in England at the present time is virtually very much the state of criticism itself*', one of being so much in abeyance. He seemed distressed that the critics had not been more severe on the young novelists and saw advancing democracy flooding the world with second rate fiction. For once he conceded a definition of what precisely he meant by *The New Novel*: '*An appetite for . . . a sharper specification of the signs of life, of consciousness, of the human scene and the human subject in general, than the three or four generations before us had been at all moved to insist on.*' Privately Wells quarrelled with the word '*sharper*'. Deeper perhaps, rougher even, less conventional certainly, but sharper—what did it mean? Given anything resembling definition as always with Henry James, he said, one required more definition.

Having paid some qualified tribute to Arnold Bennett, James' article turned to Wells. '*. . . What are we to say of Mr Wells who, a novelist very much as Lord Bacon was a philosopher, affects us as taking all knowledge for his province, and as inspiring in us to the very highest degree the confidence enjoyed by himself—enjoyed, we feel, with a breadth with which it has been given no one of his fellow craftsmen to enjoy anything. If confidence alone could lead [us] utterly captive we should . . . be huddled in a bunch at Mr Wells' heels— which is indeed where we are abjectly gathered so far as that force does operate.*'

If this seemed the supreme piece of literary conjuring, the compliments changing colour in mid-air and reaching earth before a dazzled audience, transformed, there were other phrases which could be mistaken for praise, and were less involved. '*The composition, as we have called it, heaven saving the mark, is simply at any and every moment "about" Mr Wells' general adventure; which is quite enough while it preserves, as we trust it will long continue to do, its present robust pitch.*'

Wells protested. Privately not publicly. It was not only that one phrase seemed to him to overlay and cancel out another until several contradictory meanings could be read into them; it was also being lumped with a lot of younger writers of questionable quality, until the very catalogue reduced him. The catalogue included Maurice Hewlett, Hugh Walpole and Gilbert Cannon. But it was James' joint criticism of Wells and Bennett which finally annoyed H. G. They squeeze out, James wrote, 'to the utmost the plump and more or less juicy orange of a particular acquainted state and letting this affirmation of energy, however directed or undirected, constitute for them the "treatment" of a theme . . .'

A gap in their correspondence followed. Inevitably James was shocked by the earthquake of war and its disruption of individual values, but he never betrayed his faith and continued to believe that we could only come at the inner core of life through individual self-revelation brought to a pitch of artistic perfection. To Wells this was nonsense. He knew himself as the victim of forces outside his control, and it was the final vanity to look inside himself for the key to it all. He plunged into writing and talking and before very long was indistinguishable in some of his statements from the veriest jingo. James preserved a certain detachment occasionally broken in the smoking room of the Reform Club, but quite free from the flying phrases which so quickly involved Wells in half a dozen quarrels.

Disparities of age were now underlined. James at 71 had become the avuncular figure one sees in the photographs, walking the garden with Mrs Humphrey Ward, his paunch a great sloping down from Parnassus, the watch-chain climbing across its comfortable slopes, the big black hat almost obscuring his vision, the stance of immense dignity. This was the James Hugh Walpole described as: *'A quite legendary figure, a sort of stuffed waxwork from whose mouth a stream of coloured sentences, like winding rolls of green and pink paper, are for ever issuing.'* Wells at 48 was a tubby, ebullient little man, his eyes twinkling with life, his temper short, his words explosive and more direct than ever. If both were now great figures, so far as the masses were concerned, Wells completely overshadowed James.

Suddenly, out of nowhere, one year after war began, Wells published a book which had been brewing for years. *Boon* it was called and carried the sub-title '*Being a First Selection from the Literary Remains of George Boon. . . . Prepared for publication by Reginald Bliss, with an Ambiguous Introduction by H. G. Wells. . .*' The main part of *Boon*—*The Mind of the Race* and *the Wild Asses of the Devil*—had been written four years before in a mood of discomfiture, but later chapters carried a more contemporary ring. No one was deceived about its real authorship. Earlier versions of the book made no more than passing reference to James, but the appearance of the article in *The Times Literary Supplement, The Younger Generation*, had driven Wells to add an entirely new chapter, Of Art, Of Literature, Of Mr Henry James.

One warm July morning, Henry James entered his beloved Reform Club in a mildly contented state. It was now, for him, a club full of ghosts, with special corners and chairs no longer occupied by men he had known for years, but he continued to visit it with some regularity. The Club porter said he had a package for Mr James and put into his hands what was obviously a book. He opened the package and found a slip of paper, conveying the author's compliments. He turned swiftly through the first few chapters and came to one headed, 'Of Art, Of Literature, Of Mr Henry James'. No one knows where he took the book to read the chapter, but read it he did with growing horror. His reaction, when he came to the brilliant little parody of an imaginary conversation between George Moore and himself, is not difficult to imagine. James was represented labouring '*through the long cadences of his companion as an indefatigable steam tug might labour endlessly against a rolling sea*', involving every statement in elaborate parentheses, while George Moore pressed on to describe '*with an extraordinary and loving mastery of detail . . . a glowing little experience that had been almost forced on him at Nismes by a pretty little woman from Nebraska, and the peculiar effect it had had, and particularly the peculiar effect that the coincidence that both Nebraska and Nismes began with an N and end so very differently, had had upon his imagination. . . .'*

Worse followed. *Boon* dealt with James' articles on the *New Novel. . . . 'If the novel is to follow life it must be various and discursive. Life is diversity and entertainment, not completeness and satisfaction. . .'.* James '*sets himself to pick the straws out of the hair of life before he paints her. . . . The only living human motives left in the novels of Henry James are a certain avidity and an entirely superficial curiosity. . . .*

'*Having first made sure that he has scarcely anything left to express, he then sets to work to express it, with an industry, a wealth of intellectual stuff that dwarfs Newton. He spares no resource in the telling of his dead inventions. He brings up every device of language to state and define. Bare verbs he rarely tolerates. He splits his infinitives and fills them up with adverbial stuffing. He presses the passing colloquialism into his service. His vast paragraphs sweat and struggle; they could not sweat and elbow and struggle more if God Himself was the processional meaning to which they sought to come. And all for tales of nothingness. . . .*' As for his actual characters—'*These people cleared for artistic treatment, never make lusty love, never go to angry war, never shout at an election or perspire at poker.*' What did it all amount to, Wells asked, and then came those memorable phrases: '*It is leviathan retrieving pebbles. It is a magnificent but painful hippotamus resolved at any cost, even at the cost of its dignity, upon picking up a pea which has got into a corner of its den. Most things, it insists, are beyond it, but it can, at any rate, modestly, and with an artistic singleness of mind, pick up that pea.*'

One would have expected shocked silence from James; at least an interval to absorb the pain of the blow. But no. The very next day he wrote a long letter (July 6, 1915), to Wells, as urbane and dignified as ever:

'*. . . I have more or less mastered your appreciation of H. J., which I have found very curious and interesting after a fashion—though it has naturally not filled me with a fond elation. It is difficult of course for a writer to put himself fully in the place of another writer who finds him* *extraordinary futile and void, and who is moved to publish that to the world. . . .*

' *. . . However, there are too many things to say, and I don't think your chapter is really enquiring enough to entitle you to expect all of them. The fine thing about the fictional form to me is that it opens such widely different windows of attention; but that is just why I like the window so to frame the play and the process!'*

It was a model of artistic restraint, despite a reference to '*the collapse of a bridge which made communication possible*'.

Michael Swan has said that Wells' original reply to this letter has vanished, and Swan quoted, in his *Cornhill* article, this draft:

'*My Dear James,*

'*You write me so kind and frank a letter after my offences that I find it an immense embarrassment to reply to you. I have set before myself a gamin-esque ideal, I have a natural horror of dignity, finish and perfection, a horror a little enhanced by theory. You may take it that my sparring and punching at you is very much due to the feeling that you were "coming over" me, and that if I was not very careful I should find myself giving way altogether to respect. There is of course a real and very fundamental difference in our innate and developed attitudes towards life and literature. To you literature, like painting, is an end, to me literature like architecture is a means, it has a use. Your view was, I felt, altogether too dominant in the world of criticism and I assailed it in tones of harsh antagonism. And writing that stuff about you was the first escape I had from the obsession of this war. Boon is just a wastepaper basket. Some of it was written before I left my house at Sandgate, and it was while I was turning over some old papers that I came upon it, found it expressive and went on with it last December. I had rather be called a journalist than an artist, that is the essence of it, and there was no other antagonist possible than yourself. But since it was printed I have regretted a hundred times that I did not express our profound and incurable difference and contrast with a better grace. And believe me, my dear James, your very keenly appreciative reader, your warm if rebellious and resentful admirer, and for countless causes yours most gratefully and affectionately,*

'*H. G. Wells.*'

If it was only half a retraction it was handsomely done. But by now James had *The Times Literary Supplement* on his side:

'... *It is easier to forgive Bliss and Boon for being blind to the place of art in life and the work of beauty in the world, than for their attempts to be funny at the expense of great writers of past and present. They believe all reputations, from Homer's onward, to be founded on "booming" or on some imagined "need for great men". Even in their gibes at the successful writers of the day they remind the reader of rude little boys who put out their tongues. When they attack the great, their sense of humour is still meaner.'*

Little boys who put out their tongues. But what a prodigy of a little boy and a powerfully effective tongue. Neither Wells' letter nor *The Times Literary Supplement* review entirely placated James. Time it seemed had lost its healing balm and increased his anger:

'*My Dear Wells,*

'*I am bound to tell you that I don't think your letter makes out any sort of a case for the bad manners of* Boon, *so far as your indulgence in them at the expense of your poor old H. J. is concerned—I say "your" simply because he has been yours, in the most liberal, continual, sacrificial, the most admiring and abounding critical way, ever since he began to know your writings: as to which you have had copious testimony. Your comparison of the book to a waste-paper basket strikes me as the reverse of felicitous, for what one throws into that receptacle is exactly what one doesn't commit to publicity and make the affirmation of one's estimate of one's contemporaries by. ... Nor do I feel it anywhere evident that my "view of life and literature" or what you impute to me as such, is carrying everything before it and becoming a public menace—so unaware do I seem, on the contrary, that my products constitute an example in any measurable degree followed or ... successfully pleaded: I can't but think that if this were the case I should find it somewhat attested in their circulation—which, alas, I have reached a very advanced age in the entirely defeated hope of. But I have no view of life and literature, I maintain, other than that our form of the latter in especial is admirable exactly by its range and* variety, its plasticity and liberality, its fairly living on the sincere and shifting experience of the individual practitioner. That is why I have always so admired your so free and strong application of it, the particular rich receptable of intelligences and impressions emptied out with an energy of its own, that your genius constitutes; and that is in particular why, in my letter of two or three days since, I pronounced it curious and interesting that you should find the case I constitute myself only ridiculous and vacuous to the extent of your having to proclaim your sense of it. The curiosity and the interest, however, in this latter connection are of course for my mind those of the break of perception (perception of the vivacity of my variety) on the part of a talent so generally inquiring and apprehensive as yours. . . . Meanwhile I absolutely dissent from the claim that there are any differences whatever in the amenability to art of forms of literature asethetically determined, and hold your distinction between a form that is (like) painting and a form that is (like) architecture for wholly null and void. There is no sense in which architecture is aesthetically "for use" that doesn't leave any other art whatever exactly as much so; and so far from that of literature being irrelevant to the literary report upon life, and to its being made as interesting as possible, I regard it as relevant in a degree that leaves everything else behind. It is art that makes life, makes interest, makes importance, for our consideration and application of these things, and I know of no substitute whatever for the force and beauty of its process. If I were Boon I should say that any pretence of such a substitute is helpless and hopeless humbug; but I wouldn't be Boon for the world, and am only yours faithfully,

'Henry James.'

Wells replied on July 13:

' . . . I don't clearly understand your concluding phrases—which shews no doubt how completely they define our difference. When you say "it is art that makes life, makes interest, makes importance", I can only read sense into it by assuming that you are using "art" for every conscious human activity. I use the word for a research and attainment that is technical and special. . . .'

It came in the end to this. Wells brutally declared—and the air about James would have shuddered to the words:

'I am a journalist. I refuse to play the artist. If sometimes I am an *artist it is a freak of the gods. I am a journalist all the time and what I write goes now—and will presently die.'*

For some time James had been suffering from the effects of a strange dietary system called Fletcherizing. One fad had led to another and he thought incessantly of his health. The doctor, when called, at last persuaded him to go back to normal eating but it was late in the day for a man of 72 to recover his appetite.

His last letter to Wells was dictated from 21 Carlyle Mansions, Cheyne Walk, on July 10. Less than six months later, on December 2, 1915, he had a stroke. Everything had gone against him. His books were neglected, his body ailing and a once appreciative disciple had launched a painful, brutally frank and, so far as he was concerned, entirely unprovoked attack on him. He had, he felt, been publicly humiliated. There were times when it now seemed to him that he no longer had a real place in this modern, vulgar, panting world.

Always watchful for signs of his own decay, he told his friend Lady Prothero, when she saw him after the first stroke, that even as he fell to the ground he seemed to hear a voice saying, 'So here it is at last, the distinguished thing!' Wells heard the news with considerable distress. Scores of friends were very upset. There was a sense in which some of them believed that a whole age had decayed and fallen into disuse with James' illness, and a whole way of life was now, with him, about to die. He lingered on for several weeks, but in those weeks I could trace no reference to Wells.[1]

---

[1] *The complete documents of this dispute, edited by Leon Edel and Gordon N. Ray, may have been published by the time this book appears.*

CHAPTER FOUR

Dr Coulton versus Hilaire Belloc

To OBSERVE Dr Coulton riding through Cambridge in the year 1930 was to be brought up in your tracks. His bicycle was old and dilapidated, his cycling full of dangerous assurance, and his clothes. . . . Given a cold nor'easter his eyes might be protected by a pair of bulbous goggles and the impression of an intellectual demon riding the blast was strong. In the summer he made further concessions to the climate. A bootlace skewered to one lapel with a safety pin held his Panama hat intact during his more audacious dashes between the traffic, and as the heat advanced, mechanical extensions began to proliferate round his head. First the home-made visor of sateen and cardboard with three safety pins somehow holding the apparatus in a state both firm and adjustable: then the handkerchief attached to the hat with two more safety pins to serve the double purpose of driving the flies off and protecting the back of his neck. Other gadgets were added or substituted according to the day's need. His daughter wrote '*His complete lack of self-consciousness about any peculiarity in his garb sprang readily from the conviction that, since he was the only sensibly dressed person of his acquaintance, it must be the others who were odd*'.[1]

Hilaire Belloc believed that he extended this principle into his scholarship. Coulton, according to Belloc, was full of the wildest notions himself, and automatically considered every Roman Catholic odd. From the start Belloc saw Coulton as a Cambridge pedant lost in clouds of learning, who never missed an opportunity of pouring venom on every Catholic head he could comfortably—and uncomfortably—reach. He never knew the other Coulton. He never knew the human being behind the cantankerous façade, so devoted to cats and so aggres-

[1] *Father—A Portrait of G. G. Coulton*, p. 117. Sarah Campion.

sively sure of his own Christian virtues. For Dr Coulton was as profoundly Christian a gentleman as Hilaire Belloc. If his acute mind boggled at certain more extreme dogmas and, while he bowed his head in prayer '*he reserved the right to think his own thoughts*',[1] he believed staunchly in the one true God.

He was also deeply respected by his students and friends at Cambridge and left an impression in their memories at variance with Hilaire Belloc's. They saw him as a generous man, a man of immense integrity, a considerable scholar, a lecturer who never failed to hold his students, and a person whose friendship was a very rich and rewarding experience. Nor, of course, was he always outrageously garbed. Very tall and very thin, when lecturing he tended to wear sober clothes of an inconspicuous kind. Eccentricities, in any case, did not interfere with the immense range of his scholarship.

Belloc, of course, stood for Roman Catholicism first and last, was wonderfully equipped to do battle, and never lost an opportunity of defending his faith. In person his massive body, ruddy complexion and powerful jaw might have belonged to a prize fighter, and if it seemed absurd that this man could be a writer, he magnificently reconciled the contradiction. Coming from the big frame, the clear tenor voice was surprising, but no more surprising than the sweep of knowledge, the economics, history, science, poetry, religion, philosophy liable to bubble and boil out spiced with wit and, whatever it might lack in tolerance, full of the very stuff of life.

Belloc had his eccentricities. He went to sea in a flamboyant way. There were times when he tried to recover some forgotten buccaneering ancestor in debate, argument or sailing. The sound of a cork popping would come from below decks when the *Nona*—his boat—was heeling over and on the verge of sinking, and his voice would roar out '*Without wine at sea, my children, we are as tinkling cymbals*'.[2] A similar refrain seemed

---

[1] *Father—A Portrait of G. G. Coulton*, p. 238. Sarah Campion.
[2] *Hilaire Belloc*, p. 55. J. B. Morton.

appropriate to those moments when Dr Coulton's words appeared to close over his head; it seldom occurred. When he did fall to singing a sea shanty it was an unforgettable experience. His clothes underlined his already striking appearance—a suit of black cloth, a cloak, a stiff collar from the Edwardian age, and gunner's half boots. He would half bow over your hand when he shook it, preserving manners very nearly ceremonial. But he could be downright to the point of rudeness and very, very blunt. English, French and Irish blood mingled in his veins.[1]

Coulton sprang from yeoman Yorkshire stock stemming back to the sixteenth century on his father's side, and his mother's family came from Lancashire. Their two so different methods can be traced to racial and psychological roots. Whatever Belloc may have lacked in intellectual reach was compensated by his powers of writing; if minutae of scholarship escaped him, he made do with the sheer reverberation of less exact statement. Asked, early in their trouble, what he would say if he ever met the rugged Doctor in the flesh, a contingency fraught with possibilities of bloodshed, Hilaire Belloc replied '*My dear Dr Coulton—I am so sad to meet you*'. Commonplace on the printed page, delivered by Belloc it acquired distinction. It was also a mild example of a quarrel which substituted tooth and claw for the weapons of Wells and James.

Some of the roots of the trouble can be seen in a side-battle which took place between Coulton and the Rev L. J. Walker, S.J., when Walker criticized Coulton's *Anglican Essays*: '*In a footnote to the very first page of his book*,' Walker wrote, '*there occur, in one sentence, no less than three mistakes which would justly be called "howlers" if one were dealing with a schoolboy. In Canon 1060 of the New Codex occurs the phrase: quod si adsit perversionis periculum coniugis catholici et prolis, conjugium ipsa etiam lege divina vetatur. This Mr Coulton translates "and if there be any danger of the perversion of the Catholic spouse or the children, let the marriage itself be forbidden even by divine law." It is really too bad: et translated as*

[1] *Hilaire Belloc*, p. 55. J. B. Morton.

or, ipsa taken as if it agreed with conjugium, and vetatur mistaken for the present subjunctive. No wonder the Church forbids unauthorized translation!'[1]

Dr Coulton replied:

'*Father Leslie J. Walker, S. J., has pointed out in the* Month *for May, 1923, three grammatical errors and the careless omission of two words in my translations. . . . On page 103, note 1, line 4, read now . . . "if there be any danger of the perversion of the Catholic spouse, and the children, the marriage is forbidden even by divine law itself . . .'* Father Walker also complains of my translation of *decreed for declar-ata,'* Coulton continued, '*which he would render* declared. *This last is a disputable question as reference to the Thesaurus will show . . . for the others there is, grammatically, no defence. . . . But the alterations seem to me practically without significance for the actual arguments which I base upon these documents. . . .'*[2]

The Rev Walker had also complained:

'*On page 107 occurs a reference to Dom Butler's Benedictine Monachism, which is printed with the Nihil obstat of Dom Michael Barrett, O.S.B. and the Imprimatur of the Bishop of Clifton. Upon this Dr Coulton remarks: "Nor is this a mere form; it means that any description of medieval monasticism which had displeased the hierarchy would have been pitilessly eliminated from the abbot's book." It doesn't: it simply means that Dom Michael Barrett found nothing contrary to faith or morals in the book, and that the Bishop of Clifton, on being informed of this, said that the book might be printed. . . .'*

Coulton was said, in private, to have thrown up his hands in despair. If one did not certainly follow from the other, then night did not follow day, he said. There was always a possibility that it might not, of course: but in England at least it seemed as customary as censorship was in the Roman Catholic Church.

[1] *Medieval Studies* No. 17, 'Roman Catholic Truth—An Open Discussion', 1924.
[2] Ibid.

Walker found better ground with his next complaint: '*In a section dealing with the Priest as Physician of Souls occurs the following:*

'*To give any reality to this simile of physician of souls we must postulate a society in which the patient is not only at liberty to choose the best he can afford, and not only safeguarded by the rules of a profession jealous for its own honour, but even more definitely protected by civil law against incompetence or carelessness on the part of the man to whom he commits himself. Yet, on these three vital points, there is perhaps no society among civilized nations which gives so little security as the Roman Catholic priesthood. . . .*' Walker commented:

'*Is not the author of this astounding statement aware, first, that Catholics are free to consult whatever physician of souls they may choose, without any payment at all; second, that the rules of these physicians of souls is [sic] at least as exacting as, if not more exacting than, that of the medical profession; and, third, that the penitent is most carefully protected by ecclesiastical law, both against incompetence and against other possible abuses? . . .*'[1]

And so it went on for six tightly crammed pages, wearisome in their detail. In a general reply of September 27, 1923, Coulton said:

'*Your criticisms touch scarcely more than the fringe of my Essay. You yourself in your letter to me of May 18 . . . describe quite correctly my "main claim, which is that Catholic controversialists are less fair than their Protestant adversaries". Yet you make no attempt to explain why the two greatest Roman Catholic writers of our day, Newman and Acton, who disagreed on so many points, agreed to stigmatize the habitual falsehood of Roman Catholic history in even stronger terms than any which I have used. . . .*

'*For my mistranslations I have already apologized. . . . I perpetrated, on a larger scale, the sort of slip which you yourself make in correcting me; for you print accipio where the pope's actual word is recipio. . . . In your letter of May 18, you maintain that these three errors of mine justify Fr Pope and Mr Belloc in their absurd claim of*

[1] *Medieval Studies* No. 17, 'Roman Catholic Truth—An Open Discussion', 1924.

comparative infallibility for Roman authors in the field of mediaeval history. Yet the strictest orthodoxy has not preserved those two writers themselves from far worse blunders than mine. . . .

'*The real difference between Roman Catholic and Protestant is that which I indicate in my essay . . . ; orthodoxy does not protect your party from fault, it only renders them practically incapable of confessing their faults. . . .*'

Father Walker had three last complaints: '*Having accepted my adversary's terms [of debate] most reluctantly have I yielded to his persistence in allowing the length of the controversy to become double that originally agreed upon. I regret that my own persistence has failed to obtain for the reader an arbitrator whose expert comment might have enabled him more easily to judge between us. . . . I regret also that by the ingenious device of a fly sheet my adversary has contrived after all to evade our agreement . . . and to secure the last word.*'

This referred to a printed pamphlet which set out criticism and reply to an agreed length, but included a fly-sheet carrying some extra comment from Coulton.

It could not be said that Coulton's blood was up. Whenever he fastened his scholarly teeth into something they remained fastened. He might growl. He might snap and shake. But not until much more developed stages were reached, did a rush of rage to the head release his teeth and set him rampaging.

He had already, in this preliminary skirmish, overrun his time. He often did overrun his time. Having carefully defined the terms of debate, giving the precise number of pages or words per person, he promptly delivered a script or letter twice the approved length and pleaded with his adversary for more room.

There were many comings and goings. Small scale exchanges were soon to lead into big ones. Much inflammatory material appeared in print. In the *Review of the Churches* for October 1925 Coulton attacked Hilaire Belloc's appeal to Matthew Paris as an authority for the Battle of Evesham, pointing out that the battle was fought after his death. Belloc replied: '*The general reader would at once agree, but that would be because the general reader did not know that the terms of the Chronicle of Matthew Paris applies to a whole body of work, part of which is from his pen, part from those of others, and part continued after his death. In the same way you might tell an Eskimo not to accept a reference to Bradshaw as Mr Bradshaw was dead.'*

Coulton later wrote: '*In his reply, he [Belloc] founded himself on patently false bibliographical assertions, which I corrected publicly at once.*'[1]

Now really roused Coulton proceeded to examine another '*piece of impudence*' practised by Belloc whereby none other than Gibbon was said to have been exposed. The '*exposure*' depended on '*a single word*' Coulton wrote '*which [Belloc] thought himself able to allege from Rufinus' "translation" from Origen*'. Belloc had said with that gentle understatement characteristic of him in moments of vehemence: this '*is absolutely conclusive . . . we may regard the matter as settled*', and Coulton answered: '*Mr Belloc . . . could not possibly have read the preface in which Rufinus warns us that his book is not only no word for word translation, but no translation at all in any real sense.*'[2] Coulton now issued one of his challenges to public debate which Belloc ignored.

Already wary and ready for the sudden onslaught from an unexpected quarter Coulton announced: '*He is much more likely to attack me in* The Dublin Review, *where the editor publishes personal slanders, refuses to print even a single word of protest, and allows the slanderer to palliate his falsehood with the mitigating plea that he wrote as a Catholic and for a Catholic public!*' Without warning, Belloc then launched another broadside, just as predicted, in *The Dublin Review*.

Slowly they moved from periodical to periodical each circling the other, sometimes ignoring, sometimes answering one another, but always in Dr Coulton's case, prepared to prolong the fight until the death. In *The Nation* for May 7, 1927, Belloc

[1] *Divorce, Mr Belloc and the Daily Telegraph,* 1937, p. 14. G. G. Coulton.
[2] Ibid. G. G. Coulton.

said that poor Coulton had so confused the issue between *'divorce'* and *'annulment'* that he was clearly quite *'ignorant of Catholic philosophy and medieval thought'*. Coulton at once replied that he, Belloc, created the confusion by falsifying Coulton's words, suppressing one clause and generally conspiring to make him appear ignorant of a distinction he had put into print no less than nineteen years before.

What Belloc now thought of Dr Coulton was plain from an article in the Catholic *Universe*. *'I want in what follows to call the attention of my co-religionists to the strange case of Dr Coulton.* . . . *I am not engaging him in controversy (as I have often successfully done in the past and shall presumably do with equal success in the future— for it is great fun) but dealing with him as a phenomenon to be examined with profit* . . . *he is most interesting as a symptom of something which Catholics in England too often try to forget* . . . *but which is a very real and, I think, increasing force: I mean violent and personal opposition to the Faith; a manifest intention to do it all the harm possible.* . . .'

He had been warned, he continued, about Coulton the Terror of Medieval scholarship, but he found '. . . *that all this was bogey and moonshine. Mr Coulton, as an historian, is negligible.*

'. . . *In the mechanical accuracy, the avoidance of misprints or the citation of exact words* . . . *he is as much a marvel as the Calculating Boy of my Father's time.* . . .

'*Yet he is no more an historian than a man throwing great quantities of stones at his neighbour is an architect.* . . .'

Coulton was at this time deeply into his third period at Cambridge, one of the happiest and most successful of his life. His children were fast growing up and becoming independent, he had the intellectual give and take of the University practically at his doorstep; his books, for so long neglected, were selling, and the world had recognized him as a considerable scholar.

The very tall, very thin figure of Coulton contrasted almost to burlesque with Belloc's massive frame, and his voice, moving so easily as it explained one lantern slide after another, was very different from Belloc's. Historians from all over the world went to visit the eccentric scholar Coulton in his rooms at St John's, frequently found him in an old dressing gown and felt slippers, and stood amazed at the array of gadgets which cluttered the fireplace, as he talked mediaeval history brilliantly. Perhaps the favoured amongst them were offered a draught of that nauseous cocoa he took so much trouble to brew—but Belloc was neither of the visitors nor the favoured.

Life was not easy for Belloc. A few years before he had written to Mrs Balfour '*with every year . . . I grow fixed in the void of my wife and my son; to this, new poverty and anxiety for the home add greatly*'. In 1925 he had written to Mrs Herbert describing himself as a '*man driven by necessity to work for more than he can live on*' and then came the phrase '*. . . so nearly at his end*'.[1] If it was only to intimates that he revealed such depths of depression they also saw a happier side of his character when he sat bottling wine, a baize apron across his knees, his strong, melancholy face set, as he concentrated in the cellar by the light of a candle on the very elaborate ritual. Or he would sit in the library of Mrs Herbert's house dictating and suddenly pull off the half Wellington boots, rush out on to the tennis court and tear round it.[2] Once he invited himself to lunch at the Sheeds'[3] and insisted on bringing his own food, a loaf of bread, lettuce, tin of bully beef and two bottles of Burgundy—only to eat the liver and bacon carefully prepared for the Sheeds. But the visits, preceded by a succession of letters, postcards and telegrams to announce his arrival, did not stem the waves of depression and a man destined to remain a very considerable figure for the next 25 years seemed prematurely conscious that he was '*so nearly at his end*'.

Nineteen twenty-nine was a gala year in his quarrel with

[1] *The Life of Hilaire Belloc*, p. 514. Robert Speaight.
[2] Ibid.
[3] *Of the publishers Sheed and Ward.*

Coulton. The air grew thick with arrows, 'misrepresentations', 'falsehoods' and indignation, until the whole range of polemic threatened to become exhausted. Here was Coulton in the *Daily Telegraph* for January quoting St Thomas Aquinas' decision that '*part of the bliss of the Saved would consist in looking down upon the Damned writhing in eternal torments*', and Belloc immediately plunging in to accuse Coulton of suggesting that the Blessed rejoiced in another's pain as such. '*We have . . . the statement . . . that Catholic theology taught the doctrine that the Blessed gloated over the sufferings of the damned. The statement was accompanied by an exact quotation of words which might deceive the reader but also by a careful omission of words which would have informed the reader that this attitude on the part of the Blessed was specifically and emphatically denied by the authority quoted. . . .*'

Coulton at once explained that extreme brevity had condemned him to omit qualifications and that the idea of the Blessed rejoicing in another's pain *as such*, '*was absent not only from my words but from my thoughts. In plain English*', he added, '*Belloc slipped a false coin into my pocket and then cried out upon me as a forger!*'[1]

Dr Coulton now began the device—later repeated—of telling readers of the *Daily Telegraph* that by sending a stamped and addressed envelope they might receive the full text of the '*whole relevant section from St Thomas Aquinas in the authorized Dominican translation*'. Hundreds of readers did write in.

Presently Belloc spoke once more from the Catholic *Universe*. In effect, he wrote, it was time that this professional anti-Catholic and the whole elaborate machinery of his scholarship was sent packing from Cambridge University. '*Here is a man occupying an official position in one of the two main official teaching bodies of the country and from that position he is allowed, without any protest that I have seen from his colleagues, or from the general Press, to blackguard and malign that religion which we flatter ourselves is now so well received. . . . What would happen to the Fellow of an*

[1] *Divorce, Mr Belloc and the Daily Telegraph*, 1937. G. G. Coulton.

*Oxford or Cambridge College who reviled . . . the modern exponents
of anti-Catholicism. He would be out of his job in a week. . . .'*

Part of Coulton's reply on March 15 was very nearly polite.
*'The fact is that, this term, I happen to have five Roman Catholic
clergy in my different classes here, all of whom come either by their
own choice or by that of their [Roman Catholic] directors. . . . Any
pupil may, after lecture, discuss with me any point that arouses his
disagreement. In fact I owed several corrections of detail in earlier days
to an Italian Jesuit whom I had once in my class and who remarked
towards the end of the course: "after all the differences between us are
rather philosophical than historical. . . ." '* Coulton then grew
blunt: *'The unpopularity of his [Belloc's] Church in so far as it
exists is mainly created by him and others like him; men who are not
only bullies, but cowards. Mr Belloc knows perfectly well that he
would not dare to discuss publicly with me, here or in London, to be
reported verbatim and printed, such subjects as Papal Infallibility,
Roman Catholic and Protestant Intolerance, or the Causes of the
Reformation. . . .'*

A statistical battle over the Black Death followed. In *The Nation*
of March 10, 1929, reviewing the second volume of Belloc's
History of England, Coulton pointed out that *'he attempted to
apologize for the Reformation by pleading that the "accident" of the
Black Death had given an unfair "twist" to the word. Here, again,
he had blustered about the "silly modern academic habit" of distrusting
medieval records of large numbers, and . . . quoted as a "typical" case
of the actual Black Death effects, an alleged mortality of 57,374 at
Norwich alone. In the ensuing . . . discussion he never succeeded in
bringing the total population of medieval Norwich beyond 50,000
even by taking the wildest liberties with recorded facts. . . .'*

Coulton hammered his advantage. How, he kept repeating,
how can a population of 50,000 contribute 57,374 deaths, and
how could this be described as typical. At first there was no
answer. Then Belloc let drop an aside in the Catholic *Universe*
which drove Coulton into exclamation marks. '. . . *the famous
historian'*, Belloc wrote, *'who went wrong in his counting'.*

Autumn of 1929 brought disruption into the family life of Dr Coulton, normally a rich, varied and highly stimulating affair. The learned doctor was more than capable of relaxation at home, with one kitten sprawled on his chest and another beside him, his craggy form disposed between two chairs under his favourite pear-tree in the garden, playing records of execrable taste—Whitewashing the Ceiling—Stop Yer Tickling Jock—on a 'trench' gramophone which would have reduced the best records to banality; or entertaining undergraduates with a diligence born of the conviction that 'there is something amusing in everybody'. His sense of humour was homespun, his conscience a tremendous force, his ego a thing of granite which set his daughters *warring unendingly against the most self-willed creature we had ever known*.[1] But if he *bred in his children a prickliness which made family life even more difficult than... usual*[2] he was devoted to his daughters and when, in the autumn of 1929, one of them decided to take a teaching job in Canada for two years, he was very distressed. The whole family went down to Southampton to see her off and that was a mistake. He covered his feelings for a time with quips and information about Winchester Cathedral, but when one of his jokes fell flat, he suddenly exploded. Family rows were a fairly established feature of Coulton's family life, but on September 8 he wrote to his daughter: '*When the tender put off from your ship your mother squeezed my hand for a long time, just as she did in hospital when she was waiting for her operation ... and she sat quite happily on the quay waiting to see the last of your ship's lights ... then there was another little sinking of heart when they all went behind the forts and out westward for all those thousands of miles. ...*'

In any other person it might have added a fresh edge to his attacks on Roman Catholicism. Whether it did or not the reader can judge from an article on two books by Belloc—*Europe and the Faith*, and *How the Reformation Happened*—which

[1] *Father: A Portrait of G. G. Coulton,* p. 238, 1948. Sarah Campion.
[2] Ibid. p. 1.

appeared in October of 1929. '*Mr Belloc is nothing if not drama-tic*', he wrote, '*therefore when he ceased instructing us about the Great War and began upon Church History we became aware of a most dramatic change of front in Roman apologetics. Hitherto, all Christian Churches seemed to have one cardinal point of agreement with that spiritual Judaism which Christ came not to destroy but to fulfil; all alike had relied steadily upon Divine Providence....*'[1]

Coulton could understand Belloc's rejection of the Bible which he sometimes referred to as '*a particular printed book*' be-cause he loathed the Jew '*beyond every other creature of God*'. But by what tortured ingenuity had he replaced the word 'accident' with its rude and different implications for the words 'Divine providence' in the jungle of theological nonsense contained in *Europe and the Faith*? He was clearly much indebted to Cardinal Gasquet (who had already suffered searching analysis at the hands of Coulton).

Gasquet had written, '*It is a well ascertained fact, strange as it may seem, that men are not as a rule made better by great and univer-sal visitations of Divine Providence.*' Mr Belloc, '*with the rapid in-tuition of true genius, has seized upon this pregnant suggestion....*' Providence must now be relegated to a lowly place. '*... real Catholic history is at last being written, upon an impregnable basis; there is no god, but Accident and Mr Belloc is its prophet. The Pro-testantisation of England does not fit into his general theory of reli-gious history; therefore it is accidental. The case of Ireland fits even worse; here again, therefore, is "an accident inexplicable or even miraculous". The case of Poland which crops up presently is still less in accordance with the new theory; here then is a super accident or a super miracle....*'[2]

So with the second book under review, Coulton continued. Many years of reading and penetrating thought had streng-thened the author's conviction and the very title did homage to the god of Chance (*How the Reformation Happened*). Page four

[1] *The Review of the Churches*, October 1929.
[2] Ibid.

struck the keynote: '*The breakdown of our civilization in the sixteenth century, with its difficult saving of what could be saved, and the loss of all the rest, was an* accident.' (Belloc's Romans.) '*How was "so astonishing a revolution . . . made possible"? Mainly by "the political accident" of England's perversion. Then one other accident: the triumph of Catholicism was rendered impossible by "the genius of Richelieu", yet Richelieu was minister of the most powerful Catholic State in Europe! With this, we end the first chapter: by an historical process as fortuitous as any hazard at Monte Carlo, "the republic of Christendom is dissolved".*'

Approaching his sixtieth birthday, Hilaire Belloc had paid the penalty of an erratic life by looking older than he was, even his gigantic frame suffering from overwork, lack of sleep and no settled habits. Compared with normal men of his age his vitality remained enormous, and he continued to enthrall friends at the Carlton Bar or Hennekey's in Holborn with his tremendous outpourings. Still he went to sea, wrote, drank good wine, lived to the hilt and persisted in his habit of carrying a large clasp-knife with a cork-screw attached, the one in case at any moment he needed to cut the hunk of bread he sometimes carried in his pocket, the other to open a bottle of wine. The list of books had grown inordinately—*Avril, The Aftermath, The Catholic Church and History, Cautionary Tales, A Change in the Cabinet, Danton, Joan of Arc, The Cruise of the Nona* and *A Companion to Mr Wells' Outline of History.* Constantly rushing about, he ate irregularly and wrote anywhere on whatever scrap of paper came to hand. Preoccupied sometimes with a problem, he did not eat for a whole day and then shocked his hostess by entering her house, diving a hand into the capacious folds of his cloak, unclasping his knife and cutting ham and bread under her horrified nose. A born literary fighter, Chesterton had now referred to the '*sundering quality*' in his quarrels, pointing out that Belloc was an English poet but a French soldier. Belloc's poem *The Rebel* was, he said, '*full of hatred and violence*'.[1] And J. B. Morton wrote of

[1] *Hilaire Belloc,* p. 78. J. B. Morton.

him much later: '*The task he had undertaken as a writer and speaker exposed him repeatedly to the dangers of making uncharitable judgments, and his fighter's temperament inclined him to mis-read motives. . . .*'[1] The normal Belloc was a very different person: a delightful companion, a generous man and brilliant talker. But Coulton brought out the '*worst*' in Belloc, the worst revealed by the man who passed certain famous houses and said, '*So and so lives there—I used to go there a good deal, but I can go there no more.*' His mission in life led to quarrels, his quarrels to estrangement and sometimes he could no longer return to the houses where they took place.

Unbelievably, Belloc and Coulton met once and survived the encounter. It was at a Cambridge Union Debate[2] when Belloc and Ronald Knox were eloquently arguing, '*that history should serve patriotism rather than truth*', and unnoticed in the audience Dr Coulton bided his time to break into what was plainly an intellectual frivol. He came abruptly to his feet and said that '*there should be some method of ostracizing people who deliberately and persistently evaded historical truths*'. Belloc replied hotly, and the debate developed on somewhat personal lines.

According to *Granta* it was only the President's tact which prevented them heckling one another across the floor in the worst display of earnestness which the Union had ever witnessed. But '*the more irate the two . . . men got, the more the House enjoyed it. It was a first rate pantomime. . . .*'[3]

Presently Belloc carried his printed attacks on Coulton the historian into a position which can only be described as that of the Official Distorter. He wrote an article—'Official History— How It Is Done'—which said that the history disseminated by people like Coulton, a university Don, was officially doctored to the detriment of the Catholic Church. He wrote '. . . *this history, I say . . . runs through the whole mass of our text-books and*

[1] *Hilaire Belloc,* p. 130. J. B. Morton.
[2] November 15, 1924.
[3] *Granta,* November 21, 1924.

all the other activities I have mentioned. The air we breathe is so full of it that Catholics themselves largely take it for granted. There is one little test of this which is always worth curiously noting: it is the phrase "Roman Catholic"! That phrase is peculiar to our official system. . . . Why was such a phrase ever invented? Simply to suggest that the Catholic was a member of a sect. . . . The term is even more of an absurdity than it is a falsehood. But it is taken for granted.'

Coulton replied in the *Universe*: ' . . . *many centuries before the Reformation, Mr Belloc's church was very commonly called Ecclesia Romana, even in official church documents: again . . . every convert nowadays is compelled to swear allegiance to Sanctam Apostolicam Romanam Ecclesiam . . . and finally . . . his prime minister Cardinal Gasparri, actually made it a crime in Lord Strickland that he had tried, in Malta, to change its official title of Roman Catholic into plain Catholic'.*

The editor of the *Universe* commented: '*Unless Mr Belloc wishes to make a brief rejoinder, we will not have further correspondence on this subject.*'

Momentarily Belloc said nothing. But the same year (1934) he wrote an open letter to G. K. Chesterton commenting on official historians who '*hunt under a reading glass for every slip of press or pen; even to the dropping out of a comma or the transposition of a letter; the chance writing of Peter for Paul or the paraphrasing of a remembered quotation. Their activity, like that of guinea pigs on a lawn, has the advantage of eradicating small weeds. It enables a second edition to appear with such microscopic blemishes corrected. . . .*'

Presently he was roused afresh. He had heard, he wrote on November 16 in the *Universe*, that Dr Coulton had retired. '*It would have been better for his own reputation had he done so, for each time he makes a new entry into the field of historical controversy he comes out worse battered than the last. . . . I think this puzzles him, but I can tell him the reason: it is that he lacks the historical sense.*'

He went on to argue that the origins of the English Reformation lay in Henry VIII's infatuation for Anne Boleyn and his desire to repudiate his wife Catherine. The Papal See had first hesitated, and then refused to have anything to do with the divorce, whereupon the King had repudiated Papal authority. But now . . . *'Dr Coulton . . . has invented a totally new gambit. He tells us that the whole story was invented by Cobbett . . . then having established this miracle by mere assertion but to his own satisfaction, Dr Coulton proceeds to confirm it by calling Cobbett, Farmer Cobbett—thus emphasizing the gulf that lies between the common agricultural fellow and the Don.'*

Coulton did not reply until November 30:

'Readers must see at a glance how completely all these words which I here italicize falsify my actual [words]. On the strength of these falsifications he fills half a column with facile and cheap rhetoric of which not one word has actual application to anything I ever wrote. I knew as well as he does that Pole and Sanders and countless others had preceded Cobbett here. But Cobbett had very nearly Mr Belloc's own qualities: a first rate English style, and a vehemence which often concealed abysmal ignorance. Therefore he had far more influence upon the multitude than a real historian like Lingard. . . .

'Again Mr Belloc writes: "No one now denies—not even Dr Coulton—that the origins of the English Reformation lay in Henry VIII's desire to repudiate his wife Catherine." Not only do I emphatically deny this, but I defy Mr Belloc to produce a single respectable historian, outside the Roman Catholic church, who believes it. As to the fantastic statement that "each time Coulton entered controversy he comes out worse battered than last" —I can remember ten occasions on which Mr Belloc and I have had open controversy in print, and I should be curious if he could name one in which he did not leave me in possession of the field.'

Of course there were serious matters under discussion and wit therefore, dangerous, but there were now times when one hoped that Dr Coulton might relax for a moment and not take the situation quite so personally. No glint of humour broke through. The frosty implacable voice poured on determined to establish an ascendancy already acknowledged by his own disciples and never likely to be admitted by Belloc's.

I

For a time Belloc remained quiet as the grave, but Coulton developed a few more thrusts, people made pointed enquiries, and letters were addressed to Belloc. At last Belloc rose in disgruntled dignity:

'*Correspondents have asked me whether I intended to reply to Mr Coulton's last extravagances against me. . . . May I beg the hospitality of your columns to tell them why I do not propose to do so? My motive is this: That Mr Coulton has now become a confirmed fanatic and to attempt reasoned argument with a fanatic is worse than waste of time.*

'*A fanatic is one whose hatred of another man's religion has made him lose all sense of proportion. In Mr Coulton's case this loss of balance has led him (as it usually does in the worst cases) to a loss of decent manners in debate. He has already called me a Welsher, an ape-man, a charlatan, a bully and a liar. I cannot engage in public controversy on this level. I cannot put aside plentiful and more useful work for the sake of indulging Mr Coulton's taste in Billingsgate. It was only the other day that he jeered in a public print at my lifelong friendship with Mr Chesterton; and did so with the most repulsive vulgarity. I can hardly be expected to engage further with a man who has fallen into these habits of mind and speech. . . .*'[1]

Coulton came back once more on January 25, 1935: '*Mr Belloc cannot even write a dozen lines without gross (though of course not deliberate) falsehoods. I defy him to quote any sentence in which I ever "called him a liar". It is categorically false that I ever called him "an ape-man" and, if I ever called him a bully, it was in your own columns in view of the plain facts. I added in the same breath "and a coward" for which he himself now supplies additional proof. . . .*'[2]

Sad, sad that Coulton had nothing in him of the magnificence of Shaw. The brain a-quiver with intelligence, the memory wonderful, the scholarship immense, the integrity matchless, the case on so many points shattering, but the temperament completely lacking in that gaiety which could render the most ruth-

[1] *Universe*, January 18, 1935.
[2] Ibid., January 25, 1935.

less, easy prey for Shaw. Paradoxically, there were times when his very uprightness seemed to weaken Coulton's case.

His letter ran on: ' . . . *the reasons he now gives for refusing to argue with me, both false and true, were perfectly familiar to him when, on November* 13, *he filled a whole page . . . with violent argumentation. . . .*'

Coulton presently traced a close analogy between Hilaire Belloc and Cardinal Gasquet, believing that here he came at the psychological core of Belloc's nature. Belloc had become the '*lineal literary descendant of that papally-promoted apologist who based an important defence of his Church upon a statement of fact which, at the time when he reprinted it in cold blood, he knew to be patently false*'. Coulton believed that Belloc had perfected Gasquet's method of remaining obstinately silent, when trapped, in order that large numbers of the public should believe that there must be a less discreditable explanation of these apparent errors which their perpetrator was too proud to give. The silence of injured pride could become impenetrable. Gasquet, Coulton continued, '*was able to boast that the Church had raised him to the purple as a special reward for his historical services; and his nearest present day successor in popularity and influence, among English speaking readers, is Mr Belloc*'.

The climax was rapidly approaching. Abuse and counter abuse led now in the direction of the law courts. Not all the attempts of Coulton's wife and daughters to stop the obsessional drives which carried him from one bloody engagement into another, were any use. The family grew in turns angry and sorrowful, furious and despairing. Why did he drive himself into such rages, '*why upset even his sleep with Encyclicals, Indulgences, Papal Bulls and Infallibilities. . . . No man was worse to live with than one driven by an obsession*'.[1]

As for Belloc many sad things had come to trouble him. Dr Coulton did not know that sleeplessness and failing eyesight drove him, as far back as 1932, to write to a friend asking for

[1] *Father—A Portrait of G. G. Coulton.* Sarah Campion.

some new eyes for Christmas since the ones which he acquired when very young had turned out to be most unfashionable and not of the liquid brown quality he desired.[1] Visiting Maurice Baring or the Duff Coopers he might fall asleep from sheer exhaustion at any hour of the day. He had learnt now not to fight for sleep. It was better to lie awake, calmly accepting the long stretches of loneliness which sleeplessness enforced, than to grapple with the dark gods and find himself on the verge of fever. But long periods of life remained not merely zestful; they were ablaze with activity, some of it the result of sheer economic necessity, some of feuds and battles.

In 1937 Mr Arthur S. May, Official Principal (Ecclesiastical Judge) of the Archdeaconries of Middlesex and Hampstead, touched off the final, all-consuming outburst between Coulton and Belloc. Mr May wrote a letter to the *Daily Telegraph* containing these words: '*In the early church, divorce with remarriage was permitted.*' Fr Ronald Knox rushed into print at once, demanding evidence for this practice.

Coulton's reply was long and learned, and in order not to misrepresent him, it had better be quoted at some length:

'*July 2, 1937*

'*Since Father Knox demands documentary evidence of divorce under the early Church, you will doubtless permit me to supply it.*

'*First, as to the name. Mediaeval lawyers and theologians frequently use the term of Roman Civil Law, "divortium", which meant not only separation from bed and board, but a complete dissolution of the bond, leaving the parties free to remarry. In Henry VIII's case, both parties may be found speaking of his "divorce". If lawyers of the later mediaeval centuries unanimously explained that the word must no longer be taken in its original legal meaning, this is only an instance of the confused terminology which so often hampered mediaeval lawyers and theologians.*

'*Next, as to the thing. Pope Gregory II (731–41) publicly decided that, when the wife is a confirmed invalid, the man may remarry, so*

[1] *The Life of Hilaire Belloc,* p. 515. Robert Speaight.

long as he still supports her. This is in the early collections of Papal decrees, and Gratian was obliged to insert it in his "Decretum", the first volume of the Corpus of Papal Church Law. Modern attempts to explain it away are shattered by Bishop Hefele, one of the most learned among the Committee of Consultators appointed by Pius IX to prepare the way for that Vatican Council which decreed Papal Infallibility.[1] The Ecclesiastical Synods of Arles (314), Vannes (465) and Compiègne (750), while dissuading from remarriage after divorce, do not venture to forbid it. About 1450, King Henry IV of Castile procured Papal dispensation for marrying a second wife while his first lawful wife was alive. This was appealed to as a precedent by the Cortes in 1521. A few years later, Clement VII was willing to treat with Henry VIII on the basis of allowing him two wives at a time—Catherine and Anne.

'So much for official licence; now for the licence commonly taken by society, under cover of a nominally indissoluble bond. Bishop Jonas of Orleans (840) complains that men cast off their wives on the flimsiest of false pretexts when they have tired of them (Migne, P.L., cvi, 189). St Peter Damian (1060) speaks of "many thousands" who break the marriage laws; the wife-sick man "weaves a false line of consanguinity" and thus gets rid of her (P.L., cxliv, 283). Our own Archbishops Lanfranc and Anselm, just after the Conquest, were shocked that, in Ireland, "it is said that men exchange their wives for other men's as freely and publicly as anyone changes one horse for another..."'

So it went on, the detail steadily piling up.

Belloc was now suffering even more overstrain. In the preceding year he had published The Battle Ground, Characters of the Reformation, The County of Sussex, An Essay on the Restoration of Property and a novel The Hedge and The Horse, and was simultaneously deep in writing The Crusade. In the same year his alter ego, close friend and helpmeet in all those dangerous places where anti-Catholics lay in wait, G. K. Chesterton, had died, and left an appalling gap in his life if not his defences. Early in 1937 he had gone reluctantly to America, dreading the journey and disliking the Americans. He returned from 'a howling den of

[1] 'See my Jesuits and The Middle Ages, pp. 9, 27.'

*Middle West Americans who yell like hyaenas and are of high sim-
plicity'*—worn out by the strain of lecturing, and there in the
Daily Telegraph the incorrigible Coulton had thrown down another of his interminable gauntlets. Belloc was 67 and Coulton 79,
but if the younger man felt weary his reply showed no signs of it.

'*Dr Coulton's very long letter on the Early Church and Divorce
displays conspicuously the weaknesses of which his critics have always
complained. Though very learned in his special subject and always
accurate in his numerous references, he lacks the historical sense and
never seems able to grasp an issue.*

'*The issue in this case is simple. Did the Early Church regard
canonical marriage between baptised Christians as an indissoluble
sacramental bond or did it permit divorce and re-marriage? We all
know what is meant by an appeal to Primitive Doctrine. Believing
Christians maintain that Our Lord during His ministry on Earth
delivered certain Commandments to His followers. These Commandments must have been given in a certain spirit, and therefore require
interpretation according to that spirit. For those who reject the
authority of the Church that spirit is presumably best discoverable
nearest its source. What then was the spirit of the Early Church in
the matter of Holy Matrimony? The term "Early Church" is usually
accepted to mean the Apostolic and sub-Apostolic age. Many make
it include all the ante-Nicene period. Some would even stretch a point
and include the whole of the fourth century. To discover the attitude
of these times Dr Coulton cites a vast mass of irrelevant matter,
especially from the later middle ages and including an incident of the last
twenty years. On the relevant period he has but one debatable phrase.*'

Coulton replied on July 9:

'*Mr Belloc, putting aside my facts, explains that they are irrelevant,
and that I am unable to grasp the "simple issue", which he proceeds to
wrap up in vague verbiage. Mr Belloc can both think and write clearly
when he likes; therefore, without claiming that the issue is so simple as
he contends, I will try to state it from my point of view, and leave him
to answer that.*

'*The Roman Catholic Church claims to have a Deposit of Faith
from Christ, unbroken and unchanged essentially, though it may be*

"developed". She has gradually claimed marriage more and more definitely as a Sacrament. The "Catholic Dictionary" admits that this claim was not fixed in its modern sense even in the time of Aquinas; but let us say that marriage has now been a Sacrament of the Church for 700 years or more. During those years its theory has naturally become stricter, and more reliant upon isolated Bible texts, after the fashion of all mediaeval theology. But how about the Deposit of Faith, in this matter, for the first ten or twelve centuries? We find three prominent Church synods from 314 to 750 permitting divorce in the full sense with re-marriage. We find the same permission in a Papal decree of about 740, embodied in the Corpus of Roman Church Law. How is this consistent with the theory that Christ taught His disciples, even in germ, the modern sacramental theory of marriage and its indissolubility under any condition? How can we suppose a Pope, after seven centuries of experience, to have been so bottomlessly ignorant? ...'

The letter ran on for another two-thirds of a page. Five days elapsed. Then came this from Belloc:

'Mr Coulton accuses me of verbiage and vagueness. I should have thought that what I said was as clear as any statement could be. Let me repeat it. . . .
'Now let me add something which I hope will be equally clear. The Canon of the Synod of Arles, the XXIVth runs as follows: "Placuit ut quantum potest inhibeatur viro ne dimissa uxore vivente liceat ut aliam ducat super eam. Quicunque autem hoc fecerit alienus erit a Catholica communione."
' "It was resolved to forbid as much as we are able that a man should marry any other woman while his divorced wife is alive. Moreover, whoever does this shall be excommunicate." My authority is the second volume of Mansi, page 474. Either Mr Coulton did not know his text or he risked the chance of no one looking it up.'

Coulton also took five days to reply:

'July 19
'Mr Belloc's accusation against me is so false that I have difficulty in exposing it within the limits of your space. I rest upon a decree of Arles, which Bishop Hefele, the greatest Roman Catholic authority, interprets, as I do. Mr Belloc claims to produce the original Latin, and

concludes: "*Either Dr Coulton did not know his text or he risked the chance of no one looking it up.*"

'*I must believe it quite impossible that he himself has read the text of the decrees. They number 23; mine (and Hefele's) is No. X, to read which Mr Belloc would have had to read only about an octavo page. Then come six more, introduced by Mansi (from whom he claims to be quoting), by an emphatic warning (in italics) against taking them for genuine. In spite of this, Mr Belloc, ignoring No. X altogether, lays before your readers the text of spurious No. XXIV wherewith to convict me (and, incidentally, Bishop Hefele) of either crass ignorance or dishonesty. This seems incredible; yet it is true.*'

There followed the challenge to arbitration by any Oxford, Cambridge or London Professor Belloc cared to choose and the offer of money to make objective verification possible. Belloc replied within two days:

'*Dr Coulton is angry indeed with me for pointing out his omission to mention Canon XXIV of the Council of Arles (Mansi, ii, 474) and for suggesting that he may not have come across it. The error need not have been so great as he supposes, for if he were consulting Labbe during his work (as many do when they look up a point in Early Church History) he would not have found Canon XXIV. Labbe stops at the last of the old admitted Canons—Canon XXII, which is really Canon XXIII as well. It was Mansi who much later discovered, and gives in his work, the additional six Canons, of which XXIV is the first. It is true that Mansi expresses doubt, as he found them in only one Codex (in Cod: Lucensi) and says they may perhaps refer to another Council of Arles. The value of XXIV is that it is quite clear and supports the doctrine taught from the beginning that remarriage during the lifetime of the divorced person was illicit in the eyes of the Church. Elvira, which is certainly earlier than Arles, is equally clear (Canon IX: Mansi, ii, 7; Labbe, i, 971). Dr Coulton relies entirely, he tells us, on Canon X of Arles.*

'*Canon X is, as I said in my first letter, highly debatable. Hefele was a very great scholar, to whom Dr Coulton is naturally sympathetic because he was a chief opponent of Papal Infallibility, but even those who are not great scholars can translate three such plain words as "et prohibentur nubere"—"and are forbidden to marry".'*

Coulton now found himself in some difficulties with the editorial staff of the *Daily Telegraph*. They did not want a correspondence learned beyond most of their readers to continue indefinitely and it was quickly apparent that the limitations of a daily newspaper afforded no real possibility of satisfaction to a scholar, driven to develop his case in detail. Coulton saw the point but read other motives into their discouragement. He thought that they or their editor had acted as a passive shield to Hilaire Belloc. There was considerable coming and going behind the scenes and then this letter appeared from his pen on July 29:

'*You will acquit me of responsibility for the tardiness of this reply to Mr Belloc. He is incorrigible. But I must try to show your readers what lies behind his smoke-screen of July 20. On July 14 you printed his letter undertaking to deal with my reference to "the Synod of Arles (A.D. 314)." That reference was to Canon X, upon which Bishop Hefele also based himself. To this Mr Belloc answers: "The Canon of the Synod of Arles, the 24th, runs as follows"—then follows a full quotation, from Mansi ii, 474, which, as he contends, proves "either Mr Coulton did not know his text or he risked the chance of no one looking it up". Mr Belloc cannot himself have read through that page of Mansi. He would there have found my Canon X after five minutes, at the most, and this would have shown the absurdity of writing "the Canon," etc. He would have seen that his own No. 24 could be, at best, only one of two relevant Canons, and a moment's reference to Hefele would have shown that this R.C. Bishop and I were both relying, not on No. 24, but on No. 10.*

'*But there are still stranger things behind. If only he had read the emphatic italicised lines with which his own Mansi introduces this 24th Canon, he would have seen that this great scholar, second only to Hefele in this field, warns readers against accepting Canon 24 as genuine! It is found only in a single Italian MS., and all scholars know how recklessly mediaeval scribes added to their MSS. of conciliary decrees whatever might strike their fancy from the Canons of some other*

Council. In plain words it comes to this: I was guilty of having read the relevant and genuine text; and therefore Mr Belloc, who had not, but whose random prejudice had guided him to a spurious Canon, quotes this Canon in conclusive proof either of my ignorance or of my dishonesty! This he does with an assurance calculated to convince all candid readers who, not being specialists, have no means of judging between genuine and spurious quotations.'

Coulton now definitely consulted his lawyers. The words *'Either Mr Coulton did not know his text* or he risked the chance of no one looking it up . . . ' had penetrated a skin, which achieved the difficult feat of being both thick and thin. Certainly Belloc's words approached the libellous. Three weeks legal wrangling followed. Letters literally hissed from one to the other.

On July 29 Coulton wrote direct to Belloc: *'You will realize from enclosed cutting [i.e. my D.T. letter of this date] the complete falsehood of your accusation that you had caught me in a serious professional error. A little reflection will show you that your suggestion of dishonesty was defamatory. I must therefore request now that you will (1) retract quite definitely that accusation of error and (2) apologize no less unambiguously for your slur upon my honour. I am registering this letter for security. . . .'*

For ten days there was no reply. Conceivably Belloc was busy consulting his own lawyers. On August 10 came this:

'Your registered letter arrived while I was travelling, but I have received it and am answering it from Somerset where I happen to be at the moment.

'In order that you may not think that I am treating you unjustly, I enclose herewith a copy of the reasons for which I criticised your historical sense and controversial methods. I must, however, keep this until I return to London as I am far from libraries. In town, when I can check my references, I will post it to you.'

In due course Belloc sent the missing enclosure. It repeated his own case, taking care to admit certain points of Dr Coulton's. Belloc pressed on to repeat that nearly the whole of Dr Coulton's first letter was irrelevant. *'No one with an historical sense could speak of the Early Church favouring the remarriage of divorced persons. A learned Jesuit, to emphasize this point, met Dr Coulton with a whole catena of references, the conclusion from which is overwhelming.'*

Coulton found this last passage savagely amusing. *'This learned Jesuit,'* he remarked, *'was Fr Geoghegan of Heythrop who, when I asked him in a public letter to meet the point which he and Mr Belloc were evading, excused himself as too busy to reply.'*

Coulton, Belloc argued in turn, had himself been silent on Canon XXIV, *'giving the impression that he was either unfamiliar with that text or, as in the case of the numerous points cited by his opponent, preferred to make no reference to inconvenient evidence. . . .'* Coulton explained his silence by referring to Canon XXIV as *'spurious'*. This seemed to Belloc an unfortunate word. He preferred *'questionable'* or *'debatable'*, both he thought more accurate. Words appearing in only one known Codex were in that position. *'Had Dr Coulton written as follows: "There is also, it is true, the evidence of Canon XXIV: but it is doubtful evidence, as Mansi himself points out, because though consonant with the earlier Canon IX of Elvira, it only appears in one manuscript", he would have written as an historian and scholar.'* But Coulton seemed not to know that Canon XXIV was consonant with the Council of Elvira (Canon IX, Mansi ii, p. 7) which was certainly earlier than 314.

There followed this: *'He always seems to me the sort of man who would be invaluable as a proof corrector but is of no value as a judge and presenter of the past.'*

Coulton went away to Norfolk on holiday and did not see the next letter which Belloc wrote on August 24 until August 29 or 30. It was a little masterpiece which somehow seemed to shift the required apology from Belloc to Coulton, until it was almost as if Belloc had decided that he might strain his magnanimity to accept the apologies of Dr Coulton.

' . . . I understand he now wants me to write again in your columns that I may publicly testify to his scholarship and good faith. He has

stated by implication that he was already acquainted with all the evid-
ence, so that, of the two alternatives I put—the subject of his complaint
—the first does not apply. As to the second alternative, he assures us
that he had no intention of relying on the unfamiliarity of the evidence
to the general reader. I quite accept that assurance. The strength of his
last protest testifies that Dr Coulton acted in good faith, believing that
anyone who looked up the full original evidence would conclude that
the Early Church accepted the remarriage of the divorced. This attitude
seems to me astonishing, but that he really holds it I am amply ready to
admit. Whatever view one might take of Dr Coulton as a critic, no one
will deny his great erudition, still less his sincerity.'

Coulton fell into a fury of impotence. What was he to do
with this man? He did his best with a letter to the *Telegraph*
which the editor regretted not being able to publish. It ran:
'. . . *Any reader unfamiliar with Mr Belloc's ordinary methods would*
understand this not as an apology from him to me, in sequel to a
lawyer's letter, but as his magnanimous acceptance of some lame
apology which I had addressed to him and to you. This kind of thing
must be ended now, insofar as one can ever make an end with Mr
Belloc. . . .'

Coulton had talked at length to his solicitors. Warned that
the case might come before a jury incapable of appreciating
hair-fine disputes between writers and scholars about musty
Latin documents disinterred centuries ago, he was told that they
might easily regard it as just another exercise in preciosity, unlikely to damage anyone. Deep in the thickets of his Latin texts,
Coulton abandoned the idea of legal action and fell back on
pamphleteering, a method calculated to keep the record straight
without giving anyone much satisfaction. The great days of
pamphleteering were done. The law of libel took the power,
the ribaldry, even sometimes the facts out of the case and a pale
shadow of what was really felt, remained.

Undeterred, Coulton reproduced facsimiles of Mansi, Bishop
Hefele and Clark on the dubious Canon 24, in a long complicated pamphlet published once more at his own expense, ignored

by the newspapers and attacked by the Catholics. Mansi, it showed, believed that the genuine Canons of Arles stopped at No. 23. Coulton also showed that Hefele used the word '*spurious*' of Canon 24, the word which Belloc claimed to be exaggerated.

Matters, it seemed, could go no further. But they did. When Kingsley Martin came to write a preface to Sarah Campion's brilliant life of her father Dr Coulton, he said, ' . . . *anyone who reads your book will find plenty of other illustrations of this meticulous and conscientious unwisdom which at times amounted to sadism. . . . I don't think that his tendency to advise and moralize and stand even violently for accuracy (which is a small virtue) and truth (which is the greatest of virtues) spoiled him at all as a historian or as a teacher. But I am very glad he wasn't my father.*'

Or even adversary. Certainly Dr Coulton felt himself maligned, but his pursuit of his quarry half across Europe with a further series of demanding letters left an odd taste in the mouth. If he had rounded on Belloc in the grand manner, or finished the thing off with Olympian detachment, the sympathy which he failed to arouse, might have been his. Instead, his savage insistence on the small change of satisfaction and the appalling power he canalized to that single end, brought a curious sense of anti-climax to what had once approached a scholarly crusade.

He sent a telegram to Belloc on August 30 and received a reply from his secretary saying that Mr Belloc was abroad. Coulton asked when he would be back. There was no immediate answer. Belloc wrote on September 8, regretting his absence and the delay in replying. '*I note that you withdraw proceedings. I am glad of it, for it is a pity that any academic discussion should become embittered. . . .*'

Immediately Coulton was off again. '*Your letter of the 8th from Portofino to hand. . . . My original resolve to take you into court was not vindictive. It was because, with an adversary of your stamp, this seemed the surest way of cross-questioning you publicly on this matter which, as you say, ought to have been treated academically. . . .'* He concluded, *'I shall then know how long I must reasonably wait for your considered answer, which (I take it) will be public.'*

No reply. Coulton telegraphed on September 22. *'Do you intend to answer my letter of 10 days ago?'* Mr Belloc's secretary wrote on September 24 that he was still abroad and no one knew when he would return.

Coulton wrote off at once to the secretary. *' . . . We cannot go on like this. Please forward this present letter without delay to Mr Belloc. He can, of course, still give me a good deal of trouble; anybody can do that who is sufficiently unconscientious, evasive and obstinate. . . . I will now . . . fix Monday week October 4 as the day on which . . . I must hear from him a plain answer. . . .'*

Belloc wrote suddenly on September 28 saying that he had replied to one letter received while he was in Italy, and hoped the reply had reached Coulton. *'I have been abroad for some time, but I return to England shortly.'*

By October 5 Coulton was writing: *'It is now more than five weeks since I sent you the first of two registered letters demanding a clear answer to certain plain questions gravely affecting your literary honesty. The second was accompanied with a photographic facsimile which added precision to my questions. During those five weeks my repeated applications, by letter and telegram, have brought me only two postcards from your secretary and three brief notes from yourself . . . which neither make any attempt to answer my questions nor explain sufficiently this strange delay. . . .'*

Belloc was back in London on October 7 and at last replied from the Reform Club: *' . . . I am preparing for publication an article on your methods of controversy, doing full justice to their accuracy and erudition, but criticizing their defects. I shall send you this when it appears in print; but I cannot have imposed upon me an apparently interminable private correspondence. . . .'*

Coulton was not so easily put off. He wrote by return of post:

'In your letter posted from the Reform Club at 7 o'clock yesterday evening, the 7th, you formally acknowledge receipt only of mine

dated September 29 *and sent to that same address. Does this mean that by some strange mischance, you have not, even on the evening of the 7th, received mine of the 5th October, registered to you at the Reform Club that same evening and therefore due there by the breakfast post of October 6? I am the more interested in this question because your letter seems to betray a knowledge of its contents though you make no acknowledgement of its receipt, and evade its general purport. You say that you will not answer me now because you mean to answer elsewhere.* Will you please let me know, where? *Will your forthcoming article be published in* The Dublin Review, *which refused me even a few lines of protest against a false personal accusation for which I offered rebutting evidence from a Roman Catholic student in my class here, and which claimed the right of dealing thus because the libellous words, "written by a Catholic for Catholic readers, appeared in a Catholic Magazine?" Or, again, will you choose* The Month, *which also refuses to print protests against personal falsehoods? Or again, the* Universe, *in which you have already repeatedly taken shelter when driven out of the open field? Or some other sectarian journal? These are plain questions which you can answer in two minutes upon a postcard. To this second question, especially, our readers may most justly expect an answer; and, incidentally, it will give you a not entirely negligible advertisement for your forthcoming article. In pressing for immediate and unequivocal reply I must remind you that, even more now than when I first pointed it out to you, your actual literary honesty is here at stake.'*

There was no reply to this letter. A man approaching 80, the vigour of Coulton's language and his tenacity of purpose seemed to increase rather than decrease with the years. Belloc, too, was ageing. But if gross loss of memory had deeply troubled him on two occasions he continued to travel Europe, to live erratically, to write widely, and there was little diminution of drive, eloquence or pugnacity.

And now at last Belloc launched a full scale answer to Coulton running over 32 pages, published first in *The Month* and then in pamphlet form. It was a fine piece of polemical writing which handsomely conceded an array of small-scale qualities in Dr

Coulton, but found him sadly lacking in those elements which make up wisdom, breadth of mind and a sense of proportion. *'His judgment of human motive and behaviour—a judgment essential to writing on the past—is worthless for he has no knowledge of men. . . . By specializing on details, by avoiding large conclusions and concentrating a reader's attention on petty things he often succeeds in obscuring major issues—of which he seems sometimes never to have heard. . . .'*

Of course he was the most accurate of men. *'I am myself the more inclined to admire this virtue, as I am the most inaccurate of men, writing "north" for "south", "Richard" for "Henry", transposing order, misreading my own voluminous but very badly written notes to an unpardonable degree.'* The transposition of the word 'the' for the word 'a' was to a man like Dr Coulton an enormous blunder. He would most certainly query the statement that Christopher Columbus was 'the first man to discover America' because Columbus reached an island with other men in the boat. It was a good thing in its way; but perhaps liable to become a little childish and even boring. But then Dr Coulton didn't mind being boring; rather the contrary. Even worse, Dr Coulton could not *'get it out of his mind that his antagonist'* was *'an inferior'*. He could not *'believe that a man of average education and instruction'* was *'worthy to debate* anything *with him. . . .'* Beyond that he had a violent temper, excessive hostility and was too ready to release a stream of registered letters full of threats of libel actions, to any part of the globe where his adversary sought peace of mind. Those who received *'his telegrams and private letters, registered and unregistered, launched by lawyers or in less disturbing fashion,'* suffer *'the same fatigue as do . . . hapless editors. . . .'* It was all an awful strain.

Belloc went on to point out errors said to have crept into Dr Coulton's *Studies in Medieval History*, errors exposed by Father Thurston.[1] He recapitulated the facts—as he saw them—of the divorce quarrel. He made it clear that only one of the six exam-

[1] *Some Inexactitudes of Mr G. G. Coulton.* Father Thurston.

ples brought forward by Coulton was relevant to the Early Church; he persisted that the Canons of Arles were 29 in number and that only one, 24, dealt with the general doctrine of divorce and remarriage.

There was much more in a similar vein. Belloc continuously accused Coulton of ignoring inconvenient evidence. He complained that he had '*suppressed*' the Council of Elvira, Canon 9 of which refused Communion to the innocent wife of a divorced husband.

And so it went on. The paths had grown repetitive and tortuous beyond bearing. Nothing more, it seemed, could usefully be said. But privately and publicly Coulton fought back ferociously. The so-called errors exposed by Fr Thurston in his *Studies in Medieval History* were not in those studies at all but '*in two volumes . . . in which I expressly warned the public that I was responsible for nothing except the choice of subject and translator. If you consult page 96 of my* Sectarian History *you will see that I there expose Father Thurston's dishonesty by quoting my own exact words side by side with his. . . .*' When in the face of 'his sneers' '*I defied [Fr Thurston] to produce a single instance against me . . . as usual he slunk silently away. . . .*'

Mr Belloc had made great play with the distinction between 'a' and 'the' as though the transposition of *supposed* trivialities was the essence of his, Coulton's scholarship. In fact the 'a' and 'the' under discussion were important out of all proportion to their apparent weight. '*Your whole claim to prove me ignorant or dishonest rests on the accuracy of that word. If you yourself, when you wrote "the canon" really knew that it was only one of two, then we cannot acquit you of dishonesty.*'

What did it amount to in the end? With a display of generosity which was really an attempt at ridicule Belloc had said that he could have done Coulton's job so much better for him. None of it, he said, altered the fact that '*the one great change introduced by the Church in social affairs was the doctrine of indissoluble marriage*'.

It was some measure of the heat of the dispute that Coulton's brilliantly argued evidence to the contrary seemed to get swamped towards the end. The beginnings of the battle almost disappeared in mists of hatred and threatened litigation. Scholastically, Coulton seemed to win the day, but temperamentally . . .

CHAPTER FIVE

G. K. Chesterton versus Bernard Shaw

BERNARD SHAW wrote to G. K. Chesterton on March 28, 1907, inciting him to commit a crime of the first order: the killing of a man unknown to either.

'*My dear Chesterton,*

'*However abhorrent the ceremony . . . We must get that man killed. . . . Just think of it. Here is a wretched woman in childbed who has had the misfortune to saddle herself with a half-witted assassin—the morally pretentious assassin—the amateur judge, jury and executor all in the person of one hopeless degenerate fool who just asks for money and then shoots. . . .*'

Did Chesterton want this man to stultify in misery behind prison bars and then come out to throw himself on the woman's mercy just when his children were growing up? '*I can imagine nothing more inconsiderately cruel. . . . If Rayner is reprieved we shall have to cast lots which of us will visit him in gaol and kill him . . .*'

Chesterton smiled. Shaw at his old tricks again. Characteristically Chesterton could enjoy the cartwheels, even, on occasion, approve the theory, but never quite stomach the cheerful —if entirely false—ruthlessness implicit in Shaw's words. A murder had been committed and Shaw carried whatever legal verdict was to be given to its logical conclusion. Chesterton was never completely happy with logical conclusions: particularly when they involved—even in jest—the life of a fellow human being. That Olympian view which enabled Shaw to sweep whole armies, classes and breeds into oblivion with a guffaw of laughter never belonged to Chesterton; but regarding one another as they did across precipitous differences, they remained warm friends and even incitement to murder was permissible, with certain reservations.

They first met in Paris in 1901. Gilbert and his brother-in-law Lucien Oldershaw visited Rodin and found him busy on a bust of Shaw with the living model disposed in a chair, his arms akimbo, his frame like a ramrod, his eyes twinkling, his tongue talking, talking, talking . . . Shaw found no difficulty in over-whelming the always-ready-to-be-talked down Chesterton. Shaw had spent some time attempting to explain the nature of the Salvation Army to Rodin and now developed the theme to a Chesterton all too familiar with street corner evangelists.

Chesterton was twenty-seven and his first book of collected essays had just appeared to bewilder some and dazzle others. In the same year he had married at Kensington Parish Church. A comparatively slender young man, he was already so devoted to swordsticks, weapons and the chivalry once their counter-part, that he missed the bridal train. He had stopped on the way in order to drink a glass of milk in one shop and to buy a re-volver with cartridges in another. 'The revolver', Maisie Ward commented in her excellent biography of Chesterton, 'was for the defence of his bride against possible dangers.'[1] Incurably roman-tic, the very tall young man with 'an inclination to literature' and periods of total vagueness about the reality of the outside world was already capable of buying a swordstick because it was possi-ble he might meet a damsel in distress.

Shaw, 18 years older, could not have been further removed from such a figure. The first years of the century he had spent in the committee rooms of the old St Pancras vestry and the new Borough Council, dealing with matters as remote from medie-val chivalry as drainage, paving stones and rates, writing articles on the Boer War and Free Trade. In the mornings he plunged into writing Man and Superman, never pausing to plan in advance, giving himself recklessly to the inspiration of the moment. In the evenings he might be lecturing, reading or

[1] Gilbert Keith Chesterton, p. 133. Maisie Ward.

talking, and sometimes raising a chuckle at a beautifully para-
doxical sentence from a new young writer called Chesterton.

Later in life Shaw could not recollect their first meeting but
he was so much struck by a review of Chesterton's in the *Daily
News* that he wrote asking him '*who he was and where he came
from. . . .*'[1] Chesterton, either too shy or too lazy, failed to answer and the next thing Shaw remembered was '*his lunching
with us on quite intimate terms accompanied by Belloc*'.[2]

The friendship grew. The fame of both developed. Private
exchanges soon ran over into the public prints. Presently a publisher extracted a promise from Chesterton that he would write
a biography of Shaw but his determination to write the book
was matched by Shaw's determination that he should write a
play. Several letters passed between them. In February 1908,
Shaw launched a lampoon in the *New Age* under the title 'The
Chesterbelloc'. It first examined the origins of Wells, Chesterton and Belloc, and decided that Wells, born in Bromley, was
the Complete Lower Middle Class Englishman, congenitally incapable of understanding foreigners. Gilbert Keith Chesterton,
Shaw saw as plain French on his mother's side—'*and who his
father was will never matter to anyone who has once seen G. K.
Chesterton*'. As for Belloc he '*is desperately determined not to be an
Englishman, and actually went through a period of military service in
the French artillery to repudiate these islands, and establish his right to
call himself a Frenchman*'. Which left George Bernard Shaw himself. Having no claims to French blood like Chesterton, and being without a father distinguished in cricket like Wells, he had
unconsciously suppressed his parents and was happy to be
known as a child of his own works.

Shaw found one mistake in this analysis. It was complete nonsense to talk of G. K. Chesterton and Hilaire Belloc as separate
entities. They were in fact a conspiracy: a sort of pantomimic
Chester-Belloc. It was perfectly true that the chimera known as

[1] *Gilbert Keith Chesterton*, pp. 135–6. Maisie Ward.
[2] *Mark Twain Quarterly*, Spring 1937.

G.B.S. was '*about as real as a pantomime ostrich*', but Chesterbelloc had four legs to move with, perfecting the quadruped illusion, while Shaw had only two. Besides, he had played the game with conscience, never pretending that the marionette G.B.S. was the flesh and blood Bernard Shaw, whereas Chesterbelloc put forward its ideas in quite different terms. It committed the same crime as certain journalists of the yellow press, who cloaked personal passions under 'needs of Empire', 'the Public', 'Democracy' and many other magnificent abstractions. Chesterton never said 'I, a hybrid Superman, and Grand Transmogrificator of Ideas, desire this, believe that, deny the other'. He always said '*the English people desires it; that dumb democracy which has never yet spoken (save through the mouth of the Chesterbelloc) believes it . . .*' and so on. The Chesterbelloc, by some alchemical process brilliantly known to itself alone, became Democracy, the Catholic Church, the Life Force, the very voice of Adam and heaven alone knew what else. '*To set yourself against the Chesterbelloc is not merely to be unpatriotic, like setting yourself against the* Daily Mail *or* Express: *it is to set yourself against all the forces . . . of humanity.*' When Shaw saw the front legs of Chesterbelloc as that '*very exceptional and un-English individual Hilaire Belloc, and the hind legs that extravagant freak of French nature, G. K. Chesterton*', Chesterbelloc at once replied: '*Not at all: what you see is the Zeitgeist.*'

Unfortunately Chesterbelloc had overlooked the first principle of all pantomime animals which said that any two beings artificially reconciled as one must be very carefully paired. It could be said that both portions of Chesterbelloc were externally bear-like, but Belloc was a very gregarious bear not entirely happy until he had sniffed round the House of Commons, anxious '*to keep his property in his own hand and his soul in a safe bank*': while Chesterton . . . '*Neither society nor authority nor property nor status are necessary to his happiness: he has never belonged to anything but that anarchic refuge of the art-struck, the Slade School.*' A proletariat made up of Bellocs with training as gunners would

almost certainly fight, but Chesterton could be trusted anywhere
without a policeman or even a nanny. Chesterton was an easy-
going, friendly and gentle man who made sacrifices for others with
gracious ease; Hilaire Belloc a very different pair of front legs.

As a result, the splendid animal presented by their joint performance concealed stresses which were capable of bursting the
whole contraption amidship but for the fact that the rear legs
were constantly making intellectual concessions, if not downright sacrifices, to the front. On behalf of Belloc, Chesterton protested that he was not nor ever had been a Socialist, that he believed in the Bible story of the Resurrection, and when challenged even tried to swallow the Miracle of St Januarius. Belloc
and Chesterton did not really share the same brand of Christianity or Paganism or Liberalism, or any kind of intellectual per-
suasion. *'And that is why the Chesterbelloc is an unnatural beast
which must be torn asunder. . . .'*

Two weeks after this lampoon appeared, on March 1, 1908,
Shaw wrote a letter to Chesterton:

'My dear G.K.C.,
   *'What about that play? It's no use trying to answer me in the New
Age: The real answer to my article is the play. I have tried fair means:
The New Age article was the inauguration of an assault below the belt.
I shall deliberately destroy your credit as an essayist, as a journalist, as
a critic, as a Liberal, as everything that offers your laziness a refuge,
until starvation and shame drive you to serious dramatic parturition. I
shall repeat my public challenge to you: vaunt my superiority: insult
your corpulence, lecture Belloc, if necessary, call on you and steal your
wife's affections by intellectual and athletic displays, until you contribute something to the British drama. You are played out as an essayist:
your ardour is soddened, your intellectual substance crumbled. . . .
Another five years of this and you will be the apologist of every infamy
that wears a Liberal or Catholic mask. . . .'*

Nothing else can save you now, Shaw went on. I have done
everything possible. Now it is your turn. Your only possible re-
birth is through the drama.

I cannot trace Chesterton's reply to this letter. Publicly he did not so much reply as write another book. Where the talk had once been of writing a biography of Shaw it emerged, like all such Chesterton attempts, as an analysis of ideas. But if there was little of Shaw the man in the book, it could always be argued that Shaw himself had repaired the omission endlessly in his own books. Chesterton saw Shaw as an Irishman who had escaped his roots, a puritan completely lacking in the religious basis of that philosophy, and a progressive, the speed of whose thought continually threw him into confusion.[1] His biggest trouble was that he failed to embrace the full complexity of life and in that respect was like the Venus de Milo—'*all that there is of him is admirable*'.

In a man by nature so humane there was a curious lack of flesh and blood in so much that he wrote, thought and did. '*It was his glory that he pitied animals like men; it was his defect that he pitied men . . . too much like animals.*' A vegetarian and water drinker almost by profession this '*paleness*' crept into many of his attitudes, but there was far too much life and vigour in his utterance for it ever to become anaemic. Yet whenever great social issues were under analysis he approached them like an economist. He was detached, debonair, talking at one remove. One might almost say that Shaw disliked murder '*not so much because it wastes the life of the corpse, as because it wastes the time of the murderer. . . .*'[2]

But contradictions multiplied. When the '*progressive*' world revolted against religion it naturally allied itself to science. Imagine the shock it got when the most passionate of its high priests, George Bernard Shaw, took a long calculating look at the '*veiled god of Huxley and Tyndall, and then with the greatest placidity and precision kicked it in the stomach*'. Shaw had written somewhere '*When astronomers tells us that a star is so far off that its light takes a thousand years to reach us, the magnitude of the lie seems to me*

[1] *Gilbert Keith Chesterton*, p. 199. Maisie Ward.
[2] *George Bernard Shaw*. G. K. Chesterton.

inartistic.' Everyone—even his most devoted disciple—was left breathless by this paralysing piece of impudence. G.K.C. found it not only delightful; it illustrated a far more significant point about Shaw—'*that his apparent exaggerations are generally much better backed up by knowledge than would appear from their nature...*' He could '*lure his enemy on with fantasies and then overwhelm him with facts*'.[1]

If Shaw had his limitations he remained a great man and a genius. Through his characters he had given inspired answers to the great questions of the day, brought philosophy back into drama, recovered the atmosphere of Shakespeare, and forced a re-examination of one convention after another; but there, deeply and sharply, they parted company. Wells and Shaw were all for kicking outmoded convention out of the window and leaving the window wide enough to permit something they understood as the sweet, clean air of the future to penetrate. Chesterton said: keep our conventions—'*keep them and look for their meaning: Revolution does not mean destruction; it means restoration*'.

With which inevitable excursion into paradox we had better turn back to Bernard Shaw. He could not resist reviewing the book. '*This book is what everybody expected it to be*' he wrote, in *The Nation* for August 25, 1909, '*the best work of literary art I have yet provoked ...*'.

G.B.S., he continued, was a soul of infinite worth. Everyone knew that; not least his present biographer, Chesterton. But in some respects the book was hopelessly misleading: '*... everything that he could have ascertained easily by reading my own plain directions on the bottle ... remains for him a muddled and painful problem solved by a comically wrong guess.*'

As an account of his doctrine, Chesterton's book remained to Shaw, '*either frankly deficient and uproariously careless or ... madly wrong*'. Not only doctrine; biographically also it had sad moments; but neither Shaw nor Chesterton were people

[1] *George Bernard Shaw.* G. K. Chesterton.

bothered by microscopic accuracy to the exclusion of the spirit of the thing. Unfortunately Chesterton found no small part of his spirit in beer, Shaw said. '*Teetotalism is, to Mr Chesterton, a strange and unnatural asceticism forced on men by an inhuman perversion of religion. Beer drinking is to him, when his imagination runs away with him on paper, nothing short of communion.*' Shaw didn't drink beer for two reasons. The first was obvious—he did not like it; the second—his profession enforced a state of critical training and beer was fatal both to training and criticism. Mr Chesterton on these issues protested too much. Was a man to live on his [Shaw's] work and then protest that he '*was not drunk enough to do it properly*'?

And look at all this stuff about Calvinism. Because Shaw perceived '*that once a man is born . . . you may educate or form his character until you are black in the face and he is still predestinate*'—Chesterton concluded that he was a Calvinist. A moment later '*Chesterton is Calvinistically scorning me for advocating Herbert Spencer's notion of teaching by experience. . . .*' What—in flawless bad grammar—was one to do with this fellow?

Book and review appeared almost simultaneously with Chesterton moving to Beaconsfield and an undated letter to Shaw began: '*Dear Bernard Shaw, I trust our recent tournaments have not rendered it contrary to the laws of romantic chivalry . . . for me to introduce to you my friend Mr Pepler, who is a very nice man indeed though a social idealist. . . .*'

Shaw replied on October 30: 1909. '*. . . Chesterton—Shaw Speaks—Attention—I saw your man and consoled him spiritually; but that is not the subject of this letter. . . .*' The biography, Shaw went on, must have been founded on a hazy '*recollection of a five-year-old perusal of* Man and Superman', it contained such a lot of fearful nonsense; but that, again, was not the subject of his letter. He wrote for one reason and one reason only—where was that play? A play should contain about 18,000 words and if Chesterton managed to get paid at a rate which Massingham once considered grossly extortionate for Shaw's own work—

£3 a 1,000 words—he would get £54. '*Let us assume that your work is worth twice as much as mine; this would make £108. . . .*'

Extraordinarily, Shaw had taken the trouble to write a scenario specially for Chesterton, running to many pages which are still unpublished. It dealt with the return of St Augustine to the England he remembered converting, and promised to be highly sympathetic to Chesterton. The scenario now resides amongst the collection of literary remains treasured by Dorothy Collins. Chesterton never completed the play.

Shaw even offered to come over to Beaconsfield in his motor car, to give a hand with the words; but nothing would persuade Chesterton to embark upon that particular play. To any established modern writer, the sum of £108 for an original play may sound absurd, but in 1908 Chesterton had sold his book *Orthodoxy* outright for £100, and until his affairs were taken over by A. P. Watt & Son, was continuously at the mercy of publishers he never troubled to criticize. Large, fat, comfortable, generous, Chesterton was the perfect prey for any predatory publisher and when he did at last complete a play called *Magic*, once more he sold it for a song. Shaw wrote to Mrs Chesterton: '*in Sweden where the marriage laws are comparatively enlightened I believe you could obtain a divorce on the ground that your husband threw away an important part of the provision for your old age for twenty pieces of silver. . . .*'

Correspondence, talks, meetings ran on; philosophical differences remained; but no matter how divergent, angry, or opposite their attitudes, the quarrel never fell into bitterness. Ideal enemies, one came bursting out of his Socialist trenches where everything was planned, to caper along the parapets deliberately firing off volley after volley of blank ammunition, and the other laboriously heaved himself off his Distributist pallet to throw any number of beautifully fashioned daggers, roaring with laughter when they rebounded. But the quarrel was serious, sustained and at root irreconcilable.

How could it be otherwise. Here was Shaw believing Man's

environment to be more important than religion in moulding his soul; Shaw talking blithely of the proletariat taking over the ownership of the means of production, exchange and distribution; Shaw conjuring with economics until Chesterton's head swam; Shaw believing that landlords were robbers, that women must be emancipated and men so organized that they could challenge their bosses; Shaw looking for the golden age in the sparkling air of some unborn future; and Chesterton convinced that we must step back to the Middle Ages where a Catholic Socialist state would somehow overcome the pestilence and poverty which troubled those days; Chesterton believing in God, miracles and divine grace; Chesterton convinced that the redistribution of parcels of land to each man would satisfy his instinct for property and purpose in life; Chesterton seeing women as beings quite apart from men; Chesterton devoted to an Elizabethan zest for living while Shaw enjoyed some chilly pinnacle of puritanical sunshine. That they were able to communicate at length without explosion was surprising, but within the subtle satisfactions which quarrelling offers, they understood one division unknown to the rest. Blistering abuse was upholstered. Shaw's guffaw, Chesterton's bulk, continuously interposed. For the first time in these quarrels *both* men were pastmasters of the gay diatribe.

'*I hear many people*' [Chesterton wrote], '*complain that Bernard Shaw ... mystifies them. I cannot imagine what they mean; it seems to me that he deliberately insults them. His language, especially on moral questions, is generally as straight and solid as that of a bargee and far less ornate and symbolic than that of a hansom-cabman. The prosperous English Philistine complains that Mr Shaw is making a fool of him. Whereas Mr Shaw is not in the least making a fool of him, Mr Shaw is, with laborious lucidity, calling him a fool. G.B.S. calls a landlord a thief; and the landlord, instead of denying or resenting it, says "Ah, that fellow hides his meaning so cleverly that one can never make out what he means, it is all so fine spun and fantastical."*

G.B.S. calls a statesman a liar to his face, and the statesman cries in a kind of ecstasy, "Ah, what quaint, intricate and half tangled trains of thought! Ah, what elusive and many coloured mysteries of half meaning!" I think it is always quite plain what Mr Shaw means, even when he is joking, and it generally means that the people he is talking to ought to howl aloud for their sins. But the average representative of them undoubtedly treats the Shavian meaning as tricky and complex when it is really direct and offensive. He always accuses Shaw of pulling his leg, at the exact moment when Shaw is pulling his nose.[1]

The first big public 'debate' between them in person took place at Cambridge in 1911, when Shaw and Chesterton addressed The Heretics [Club]. Chesterton's performance as a lecturer could be highly original. In the first place, he found the utmost difficulty in remembering where and at what time he had to lecture. In the second he often arrived puffing and blowing like a distressed whale, hopelessly late and not altogether repentant. Not infrequently he started by saying he had not prepared the lecture and sometimes ran off into tiresome generalities. If he had prepared it, his notes took the form of a dozen ill-assorted scraps of variously shaped paper, scrawled over in pencil, chalk and ink of every hue. Their disorder was supreme. Surveying this incredible mosaic through crooked pince-nez, with screwed up eyes, he would suddenly sigh, scrap the lot and just plunge into talk. He made far too many jokes about his size, but certainly it deserved some mention since he towered over other men and achieved a Falstaffian girth no one had ever dared to measure. His voice was high and not very penetrating. Given a microphone he sometimes thrust his notes between himself and the microphone, successfully muffling it. There was the supreme moment when they gave him a gold-chased period chair which, as he made his point with some show of vigour, slowly subsided under him. As it approached the floor, without breaking his disquisition, he slipped out of it into another more sturdy one, and continued talking

[1] *George Bernard Shaw*, pp. 82–3. G. K. Chesterton.

as though changing chairs was an inevitable part of his performance. In the end he never failed to be witty, entertaining, eloquent, and full of infectious good cheer.

Shaw's method is familiar—the tall, angular body held upright with military discipline, the arms sometimes akimbo, the eyes flashing, the gestures becoming vigorous, a great stride marking a climax which threatened to carry him down into the audience, and his voice full of rich undertones, of oaths waiting to explode but never—in public—quite exploding.

It was Shaw who opened the debate and the following day the *Daily Express* recorded:

CHRIST A FAILURE

Extraordinary Speech by Mr G. B. Shaw

'*...in the course of his remarks* [Bernard Shaw] *said "When Charles Darwin came along with this theory of Natural Selection, the people jumped at it and kicked God out of the window ...."* '

The Express telegraphed Shaw asking whether he had used the words '*Christ was a failure*' and Shaw wired back: '*Have not seen report, but the fact you mention is sufficiently obvious in the modern smart sense of the word ....*'

This was too much for that august organ *The Academy*. Under the headline 'A Detestable Outrage' it wrote: '*The question whether Mr Shaw has beliefs or none may interest an egregious egotist ... our protest is against the dissemination of poisonous theories among young persons ... but we do not observe that the lecturer was kicked out of the window or that he was thrown into the Cam ... It is unnecessary to resort to coarse profanity to teach the doctrines of materialism. ....*'

Shaw had in fact begun his talk by saying that The Future of Religion[1] was a serious enough subject but of little interest to Heretics—if the word fell within normal definitions. Those

---

[1] So far as I could trace there are only two remaining records of this debate, one in Miss Dorothy Collins' collection and another in the *Cambridge Daily News,* May 30, 1911.

who really mattered in such discussions were the nice, the orthodox, the well worth while, who could not conceive why the question should arise at all. He compared a Heretic to a man with mechanical genius who began tinkering with a bicycle or motor car and converted it into something quite different. Such a man was a heretic in mechanics; 'he had a mind and a genius which enabled him to choose for himself. The Heretic was the sort of person who, no matter what religion was supplied at the' local church, would reshape it until the contraption resembled his own requirements. 'The Heretic was really a man with a home-made religion' and if men had such creative powers there was no need to worry about them; the people they needed to trouble about were the masses who took religion as it was served.

Chesterton answered this at its facetious level. Shaw seemed to believe—extraordinary man that he was—'that Heretics were people who found a machine such as a motor car', and by a series of brilliant improvizations converted it into something very different. For his part Chesterton did not mind anyone stumbling upon the endless sewing machines which always seemed to be lying about and converting them into bicycles; or, if they came across a theodolite, transforming it with a few rapid touches into a motor car; 'but he strongly objected to their finding a bicycle, turning it into a sewing machine and then trying to ride the sewing machine'.[1] Approximately this represented Shaw's confused view of religion.

Shaw continued: If people wanted to achieve a workable religious system they really must find a God they could understand. It was no use falling back on the old threadbare evasion that God was beyond their comprehension. 'The man who said he believed in God and did not understand' whatever arose in divine communication 'had much better become' a good practical atheist at once ... An Agnostic was only an atheist without the courage of his convictions. Far better to come out flatly against

[1] *The Cambridge Daily News*, November 18, 1911, and a pamphlet privately printed for the Cambridge Heretics.

God than to haggle over one's chances of redemption by remaining agnostic. The down-to-earth practical use to which a God could be turned was the establishment of laws and moralities based upon what the faithful supposed to be the will of God, and if they failed to comprehend's God's purpose how could they ever do anything of the kind. . . .

The most extraordinary paradox of modern religion, Shaw went on, was that such a fertile breeding ground as Western Europe had failed to produce a fundamental religion of its own. It not merely permitted an oriental nucleus to suppress any European substitute, but accepted a series of legends which really must be swept away before any sane man could come within a mile of Christianity. Those gullible enough to believe the story of the Gadarene swine would believe anything, and anyone accepting the story of Elisha was liable to worship the most improbable images: they, as a critical force, must be left out.

If the truth be known, religion based upon the proliferation of pointless legends, virtually went out with the Middle Ages. Hitherto the victims of idolatry, we had converted people into idols and resorted to that brand of stage management which carried certain men to the head of affairs (sometimes vigorously self-propelled) and permitted them to wear crowns or gold lace, if they were not ceremonially appointed to special chairs. These people were frequently idols at one remove, second-hand divinities who said: 'I am the agent of the will of another idol. I understand his will and hand it on to you.' To make the distinction more convincing *we generally had to give them such a different income from our own that their way of life* was *entirely removed from that of the multitude*.[1]

Now modern democracies were trying to lift human nature to the point where such legends and second-hand divinities became repugnant. In revolutions like the French, 'democracy went first to the cathedral and knocked the heads off the idols of

[1] *Cambridge Daily News,* May 30, 1911.

stone. Nothing happened. No crash of thunder stunned the universe and the veil of the temple remained intact.' Encouraged they proceeded 'to the palaces and cut off the heads of the idols of flesh and blood. Still nothing happened ...' We were, in fact, gradually getting rid of more and more idols and in future we would have to put before democratic people a practical form of religion which avoided the flagrant contradictions inherent in Christianity. Presently came the blasphemy wrongly reported in some newspapers. Shaw did not say God was kicked out of the window. He said that with the appearance of Darwin *'the old idea of God was banished from the world'*.

Chesterton replied: *'He would emulate Shaw's blasphemy, because he thought it was an easy game ... if ever God died it was in the middle of the eighteenth century. It now remained for Mr Shaw to explain why God had risen from the dead'* and why Shaw had found it necessary to *'use the term God in order to excite a modern audience'*.[1]

Mr Shaw said *'that democracy meant the destruction of idols. Of course it was characteristic of Shaw that he knew no more what democracy meant than he* [Mr Chesterton] *knew'* Chinese. *'Democrary meant a very simple thing.'*

It meant that 'if they were snowed up' in this lecture room, 'which for the purposes of debate he hoped they might be', everyone would have a say in what should be done. If, for example, they 'raided the platform and killed him', or put a Gatling gun on the table, or tried 'any of the other forms of human government', it would be a majority decision. In a word, democracy need have nothing to do with the destruction of idols.

Mr Shaw stated that *'when the French revolutionaries marched'* they *'first cut off the heads of the idols in the cathedrals'*. They certainly did not. *'What they did was to declare a number of very rigid'* and, he thought, *'largely true metaphysical dogmas'*, before a very natural quarrel with the aristocracy led them to believe that they had been sold to the enemy, whereupon they *'cut off the*

[1] *Cambridge Daily News,* November 18, 1911.

heads of the idols of flesh and blood'.[1] Shaw, as usual, was talking his own inspired brand of erratic nonsense.

Shaw next proclaimed, with violent gestures and a powerful relapse into an Irish accent, that he was a mystic and believed the Universe to be driven by what, for convenience, he would call a Life Force. *'To attempt to present this particular will or power as God—in the former meaning of the word—was now'* quite hopeless. The sort of God he envisaged—if it could be called a God—did not possess a brain like ours and used a means of communication far less tangible and more complex. But he had created us in order to be able to use us, and this led Shaw into a statement which Chesterton found the final outrage. *'We were,'* said Shaw, *'experiments in the direction of making God.'* There followed a brief explanation, distinguished by a mystical concentration only intelligible to the very deeply initiate. What God, said Shaw, was doing, amounted to this: from being a powerless will or force he was creating Himself. *'We were'* in ourselves *'not very successful attempts at God,'* but the Life Force had implanted the ideal of God in our minds, and Shaw believed that if we could make this fully conscious and realize that *'there would never be a God unless we made one'*, we should be moving in the right direction. We were the instruments by which the ideal *'was trying to make itself a reality'*. Working towards that ideal we might become super-men and continue reaching towards different orders of being, until we were transformed into a world of organisms who had literally achieved God.[2]

Chesterton—in reply—joyfully embraced the principle that we must have a God of some kind since we needed a purpose in the Universe; but this indefinable deity struggling to exist in a material world—oh dear, oh dear—where was the logical Mr Shaw landing himself? In the first place, *'there was no such thing as trying to exist'*. We *'had to exist before'* we tried. Logical difficulties apart there remained no value whatever in the kind of

[1] Pamphlet privately printed for the Cambridge Heretics.
[2] *Cambridge Daily News,* May 30, 1911, and privately printed pamphlet.

God Shaw envisaged, because what we first needed was '*something fixed in a God by which we regulated ourselves*. . . .' Instead of bluntly admitting his atheism, Shaw preferred to think that some mysterious deity was '*struggling at the bottom of the universe*' and would gradually materialize in a medium combining matter and spirit in just the right proportions to show that Mr Shaw was right. But supposing Shaw had said—'*Here are five poor children. They haven't got a mother; let them all come together and manufacture a mother*—' he thought his audience would agree that there was a certain well-known slip in the logic. Of course, if any unfortunate family desired to deceive itself deeply enough in the interests of survival by calling its eldest child mother or God—Chesterton did not mind in the least. He simply doubted whether it would advance man's religious life very much.

Chesterton did not like all this shilly-shallying. '*If he had to choose between Shaw's gospel and that of*' an out-and-out atheist like '*Charles Bradlaugh, he would pray—with the greatest disapproval of Bradlaugh*'—that he might be admitted into his camp.[1]

October of the same year saw yet another debate under discussion between them and Shaw wrote:

'*My dear G.K.,*

'*With reference to this silly debate of ours, what you have to bear in mind is this.*

'*I am prepared to accept any conditions. If they seem unfair to me from the front of the house, all the better for me; therefore do not give me that advantage unless you wish to, or are—as you probably are—as indifferent to the rules as I am. . . .*

'*Did you see my letter in Tuesday's* Times? *Magnificent! My love to Mrs Chesterton and my most distinguished consideration to Winkle.*[2]

'*To hell with the Pope!*

'*Ever, G.B.S.*'

[1] *Cambridge Daily News,* November 18, 1911, and privately printed pamphlet.
[2] Mr Chesterton's dog.

At lunch together one day shortly afterwards in London, Shaw said to Chesterton: 'I'm a likeable old rascal you know—but you really must stop poisoning my mind with all these heresies about God. Otherwise I shall really have to go for you.'

A spasm of merriment began in Chesterton's stomach, spread to his chest, shook his shoulders and finally threw his head back with a glorious gurgle of delight. 'It's your intellectual magnanimity which destroys me', he said at last. 'If only you were a nasty fellow who lost his temper.'

Shaw: 'Have you ever lost yours?'

Chesterton sighed: 'I've searched hard and long. It just doesn't seem to be there.' 'Then for God's sake', Shaw boomed, 'cultivate one. You'll never win an argument with me until you're raving—plain, mad, bull-at-a-gate raving—with temper.'

Seen together walking down the street they made a wonderful pair. Both tall, powerfully built men, Chesterton's mode of locomotion was given a certain sway by his immense girth, his black cape swinging in the wind like the sails of a ship, while Shaw's military stilts took him along at a cracking pace which Chesterton quickly pleaded should be slowed in order that he had breath enough to talk. The high voice alternated with the rich Irish cadences, the great oaths from Shaw brought mild remonstrances, the long sentences from Chesterton were punctuated by wheezy rumbles of laughter, both men continuously hovering on the edge of their two so different brands of wit.

In the early stages of the war serious illness overtook Chesterton. As usual he was working ferociously. Giving the impression that he had all the time in the world, always gentle and considerate, when involved in a major book, he worked from 10 in the morning till 1, from 2.30 to 4.30 and from 5.30 to 7.30. He drank rather more than usual in these years and there were times when his friends felt he had come—almost absent-mindedly—to depend on the stimulus of wine to sustain the torrential output. Worries about his brother involved in a libel

suit, overwork and the outbreak of war combined to produce
this illness. Dr Pocock came to visit him, found the bed partly
broken under his leviathan bulk, and said to Chesterton, his
head lying lower than his body: 'You must be horribly uncomfortable.'

'Why now you mention it—I suppose I am,' said Chesterton
with no more emphasis than a man saying good morning.[1]

The illness lasted several months and reached a stage where
he ceased to recognize his wife Frances, and in January 1915
drove her to write: *Gilbert remains much the same in a semi-
conscious condition . . . I feel absolutely hopeless.*

In June of 1914 Shaw had offered him money. *You won't
hurt me as I have just now an unnecessarily large . . . balance . . .*' In
January of the following year he again asked after Chesterton's
health. Presently he wrote from Ireland saying that Augustus
John, due to paint him, had been lost on the way for a week,
arrived full of contrition and promptly obliterated three
masterpieces in a row.

He was genuinely glad when Chesterton, at last well again,
wrote to him on June 12, 1915:

'*My dear Bernard Shaw,*
'*I ought to have written you a long time ago, to thank you for your
kind letter which I received when I had recovered.*
' *. . . I do not agree with you about the war; I do not think it is going
on of its own momentum: I think it is going on in accordance with that
logical paradox whereby the thing that is most difficult to do is also the
thing that must be done. . . . I have always thought that there was in
Prussia an evil will. . . .*'

Shaw replied ten days later:

'*I am delighted to learn under your own hand that you have recovered all your health and powers with unimpaired figure. . . .*
'*It is perfectly useless for you to try to differ with me about the war.
Nobody can differ with me about the war: you might as well differ
from the Almighty about the orbit of the sun. I have got the war right;*

[1] *Gilbert Keith Chesterton,* pp. 328–9. Maisie Ward.

and to that complexion you too must come at last, your nature not being a fundamentally erroneous one.

'*At the same time, it is a great pity you were not born in Ireland. You would have had the advantage of hearing the burning patriotism of your native land expressing itself by saying exactly the same things about England that English patriotism now says about Prussia, and of recognizing that though they were entirely true, they were also a very great nuisance, as they prevented people from building the future by conscientious thought. . . .*'

As to the will of evil in Prussia . . . . Of course it was there, but he had been fighting that evil will in himself and others all his life. What was necessary was to make ridiculous the cry—vengeance is mine—and '*whenever anyone tells an Englishman a lie, to explain to the poor devil that it is a lie, and that he must stop cheering it as a splendid speech . . .*'

Shaw concluded with a reference to his pamphlet *Uncommon Sense About the War*. Someone had stolen his title. He would have to call it *More Common Sense About the War*. Chesterton's reaction to this pamphlet took the form of a remonstrance gentle out of all proportion to the dangerous document inciting it. Half of Shaw's friends and all his enemies went into vicious attack when the contents of this 'violently anti-British screed' became known. Chesterton wrote a private, a very private letter. He hated what Shaw said. He thought the pamphlet dangerous. He explained his own views at length but even when he had completed what became a long letter he did not post it. Hypersensitive himself, he did not want to add to the storm which burst about the quite untroubled head of G.B.S.[1]

'. . . *You are, my dear Shaw, face to face with certain new facts; new at least to the "green things" of that age in which you and I began to write. But though it is self-evident that these things are new facts you still treat them as if they were old friends. . . .*'

Chesterton said he had once written of Shaw: '*I have no particular objection to people who take the gilt off the gingerbread, if only*

[1] This unpublished letter belongs to Miss Collins' collection.

for this excellent reason, that I am much fonder of gingerbread than I am of gilt. He can, if he likes, scrape the romance off the armaments of Europe or the party system of Britain. But he cannot scrape the romance off love or military valour, because it is all romance and three thousand miles thick.'

In his letter Chesterton now said that he could not find better words to describe the pamphlet of G.B.S. *'You are wrestling with something too romantic for you to realize. It is the real thing....'*

'... Your weakness touching what you call "the nonsense about Belgium", after all is simply that it is not nonsense....'

'You are out of your depth my dear Shaw; for you jumped into this deep river to prove that it was shallow....'

People like himself were supporting Sir Edward Grey's war, not because they had been tricked into a fake attitude, but because they never expected to be presented with an attitude quite so sympathetic. *'But you cannot bear to be on the democratic side even by accident: so you would rather twist out some extraordinary tale of the Kaiser being taken at a disadvantage by the hellish cunning of English country gentlemen.... Suppose, seriously, my dear Shaw, that the Kaiser's fate were put into the hands of all the railwaymen or cabmen or captains of ferry steamboats who refer to him without affection as Uncle Bill; would he not wish himself back in the hands of Sir Edward Grey ... ?'*

Gentle, gentle Chesterton. It was unfortunate, so hot on the heels of this unposted letter, to have H. G. Wells suddenly burst upon him, because Wells liked Chesterton no less than Shaw; but burst Wells did, words flying.

'My dear G.K.C.,

'Haven't I on the whole behaved decently to you? Haven't I always shown a reasonable civility to you and to your brother and Belloc? Haven't I betrayed at times a certain affection for you? Very well, then you will understand that I don't start out to pick a needless quarrel with The New Witness *crowd.*

'But this business of the Hueffer book in The New Witness *makes me sick. Some disgusting little greaser named —— has been allowed to*

insult old F.M.H. in a series of letters that make me ashamed of my species. Hueffer has many faults no doubt but firstly he's poor, secondly he's notoriously unhappy and in a most miserable position, thirdly he's a better writer than any of your little crowd. . . .'

The letter finished by saying that he, Wells, had no intention of letting *The New Witness* into his house again, it all reminded him so much of '*the-cat-in-the-gutter-spitting-at-the-passer-by*'.

To which G.K.C. replied:

'My dear Wells,
' . . . Any quarrel between us will not come from me; and I confess I am puzzled as to why it should come from you, merely because somebody else who is not I dislikes a book by somebody else who is not you, and says so in an article for which neither of us is even remotely responsible. I very often disagree with the criticisms of ——; I do not know anything about the book or the circumstances of Hueffer. I cannot help being entertained by your vision of ——, who is not a priest, but a poor journalist, and I believe a Free-Thinker. But whoever he may be (and I hardly think the problem worth a row between you and me) he has a right to justice: and you must surely see that even if it were my paper, I could not either tell a man to find a book good when he found it bad, or sack him for a point of taste which has nothing in the world to do with the principles of the paper. For the rest, Haynes represents The New Witness *much more than a reviewer does, being both on the board and the staff; and he has put your view in the paper —I cannot help thinking with a more convincing logic. Don't you sometimes find it convenient, even in my case, that your friends are less touchy than you are?*
'By all means drop any paper you dislike, though if you do it for every book review you think unfair, I fear your admirable range of modern knowledge will be narrowed. Of the paper in question I will merely say this. My brother, and in some degree the few who have worked with him, have undertaken a task of public criticism for the sake of which they stand in permanent danger of imprisonment and personal ruin. We are incessantly reminded of this danger; and no one has ever dared to suggest that we have any motive but the best. If you should ever think it right to undertake such a venture, you will find

that the number of those who will commit their journalistic fortunes to it, is singularly small: and includes some who have more courage and honesty than acquaintance with the hierarchy of art. It is even likely that you will come to think the latter less important.

'*Yours, sans rancune,*

'*G. K. Chesterton.*'

Wells wrote back:

'*Dear G.K.C.,*

'*Also I can't quarrel with you. But the Hueffer business aroused my long dormant moral indignation and I let fly at the most sensitive part of* The New Witness *constellation, the only part about whose soul I care. I hate these attacks on rather miserable exceptional people like Hueffer and Masterman. I know these aren't perfect men, but their defects make quite sufficient hells for them without these public peltings. I suppose I ought to have written to C.C.[1] instead of to you. One of these days I will go and have a heart-to-heart talk to him. Only I always get so amiable when I meet a man. He, C.C., needs it—I mean the talking to.*

'*Yours ever,*

'*H.G.*'

The New Witness continued to be a thorn which troubled Chesterton's flesh, and presently there was difficulty over an article of Shaw's. Chesterton wrote to explain why publication had fallen through. '*As you know I was myself quite eager to publish it and also . . . to answer it . . . .*' Chesterton thought the difference between Prussia and France touched on in the article, much deeper than any difference between a monarchy and a republic . . . '*and . . . in that deeper difference, Russia with all her evils (like England with all her evils) is really on the French side. Therefore I take the Alliance and its safety very seriously . . . .*' He relied on Shaw's wonderful gift of intellectual magnanimity to understand why they could not publish the article. Shaw easily survived the test.

[1] Cecil Chesterton, G.K.'s brother.

After the war, Shaw wrote another unpublished letter to Chesterton on a very different subject. It congratulated a man of Chesterton's weight for his performance on the thin ice of Shaw's love letters. This probably concerned the negotiations between Mrs Patrick Campbell and her publishers when she promised a book of memoirs, including love letters from a well-known duke, a famous painter, Barrie and Shaw, and received £2,000 in exchange without knowing the austerities of the law of copyright. Shaw now wrote to Chesterton that publication of love letters was to him equivalent to indecent exposure . . .

'*She has a right to her view and to her letters*', Shaw wrote. '*I cannot call a policemen and flourish the Copyright Act. I cannot control her (in public) even as to the miserable fiction that it was all a joke . . . . Besides, it was delightful while it lasted.*' When Shaw, Barrie, the duke and painter, refused point blank to make an exhibition of their infatuations in public, Mrs Campbell pleaded that she was now heavily in debt to the publishers and in the end Shaw and Barrie relented to the extent of permitting a few edited examples.

By 1925 *The New Witness* had become *G.K.'s Weekly*, with Chesterton still in the editorial chair. It was a period of his life when he had written some fifty books, had at least three new manuscripts under correction and was burdened with editing *G.K.'s Weekly* at £500 a year, a sum which Shaw calculated left £3 10s. 2d. a week nett and was equivalent to selling himself into slavery for ten years. Quarrelling of any kind was distasteful; quarrelling among the staff became appalling; but above all he hated the moment when someone suggested that he, as editor, should adjudicate. He could never it seems '*stand up to accusations from one man against another*'.[1] He had no idea of time and would come drifting into the office smoking a cigar, chain smoke from one cigar to another, dictate an article or two, swinging about on his small feet which, like his high voice, seemed hopelessly inadequate to his bulk. Then he would say 'I

[1] *G. K. Chesterton*, p. 421. Maisie Ward.

think I'll go now'. Sometimes he vanished for an hour, sometimes he did not return for days.

It was a harassed, difficult time for Chesterton. The paper quickly ran into financial difficulties which he sometimes met single handed, paying on one occasion a printer's bill for £500, but he remained serene and *'wonderfully kind'*. *'He never got angry. He never minded being interrupted. If his papers blew away he never got impatient.'* Thus Miss Dunham, sub-editor of the *New Witness*[1] in Chesterton's day. Shrewdly, she added, *'Sometimes his patience hurt one.'*

He was still editor of *G.K.'s Weekly* when he 'clashed' again with Shaw in public. Now the scene was elaborately laid. Shaw wrote to Chesterton on October 20, 1927, insisting that the meeting be properly organized. It was quite evident, Shaw said, that Chesterton's people, The Distributist League, had no idea of what they were up against. *'Nothing must be left to well intentioned Godforsaken idiots who have no experience or organizing power, and who believe that public meetings are a national phenomena that look after themselves. . . .'* He complained of the pre-disposal of the proceeds without consultation, and objected to part of the money going to the King Edward Hospital Fund because *'every successful commercial brigand is buying Indulgences and Pardons by pouring money into hospitals'*. The Fabian Society, he said, could *'hardly keep alive'* and *'I'd rather pay Belloc's debts'*.

Everyone is sufficiently familiar with Shaw's Socialism to understand what followed. The philosophy of the Distributist League is another matter. Official propaganda stated that it offered the only practical alternative to the twin evils of Capitalism and Socialism. This was a grandiose claim if only because Socialism at that time was quite untried and Government of the people by the people for the people as remote as the phrase was romantic. Certainly the organized worker had suddenly revealed a tremendous mailed fist concealed within the trade unions when, one year before, the General Strike had paralysed

[1] *G. K. Chesterton*, p. 421. Maisie Ward.

the whole country, but a demonstration of industrial power was very different from holding political office.

The Distributist League opposed Capitalism and Socialism because both led to the concentration of property and power in a few hands which meant '*enslavement of the majority*'. If this phrase revealed the emotional lack of definition which bedevilled half the literature of the League, everyone understood what was meant by opposition to busybodies, monopolies and the State. PERSONAL LIBERTY was to be restored—mainly by the better Distribution of Property, which meant ownership of land, houses, workshops, gardens, and the means of production. Such a re-distribution was to result from '*protecting and facilitating the ownership of individual enterprises in land, shops and factories*'. On the authority of its own literature the League fought for small shops and shopkeepers against multiple shops and trusts, individual craftsmanship and Co-operation in industrial enterprises, the smallholder and yeoman farmer against monopolists and badly farmed estates. More important still, every worker should own a share in the assets *and control* of the business in which he worked.

If these broad principles were undeniably splendid there was little indication of the machinery by which the old order was to be converted into the new. Like Wells in his Utopia, a few scrawls of coloured chalk dashed in the towers and pinnacles of a quite new way of life, exciting the mind precisely because the flashes were incomplete; but ask for the details; ask, as the eye went glinting along, how this was all to come about, what action would shake the vastly entrenched society we knew, and there was an uncomfortable silence. . . . This was one of Shaw's preliminary complaints about the Distributists.

Hilaire Belloc took the chair at the meeting which followed, and almost at once Shaw sprang to his feet and strode into his subject, eyes flashing, beard waving, arms crossed on his chest. The title given to the debate was 'Do We Agree?' and Shaw said: ' . . . *Some of you might reasonably wonder, if we agree, what we are going to talk about, but I suspect that you do not really care much what we debate . . . provided we entertain you by talking in our characteristic manners. . . .'*[1]

The secret of the attraction which men like Chesterton and himself exercised was really very simple—they were madmen. Instead of earning a straightforward decent living as bus conductors or road sweepers they went about doing and saying the queerest things. *'Mr Chesterton tells and prints the most extravagant lies. . . . I do very much the same sort of thing. . . . Obviously we are mad, and in the East we should be reverenced as madmen. . . .'*[2]

There followed five minutes witty talk. Since he had cleared his mind of the more commonplace Socialist cant (Shaw continued), he had always said: *'Don't put in the foreground the nationalization of the means of production, distribution and exchange: you will never get there if you begin in that way. You have to begin with the question of the distribution of wealth.*

'The other day a man died and the Government took four and a half million pounds as death duty on his property. That man made all his money by the labour of men who received twenty-six shillings a week after years of qualifying for their work. Was that a reasonable distribution of wealth? We are all coming to the opinion that it was not reasonable. . . .'[3]

Even Chesterton, with his very special brand of madness, might be persuaded to agree on that. *'Mr Chesterton has rejected Socialism . . . probably because it is a rather stupid word; but he is a Distributist, which means today a Redistributist.'* In short he *'has arrived by his own path at my decision. . . .'* [Loud laughter.]

One of the problems constantly arising in an organized community, Shaw went on, was *'at what point are we justified in killing for the good of the community'*. He would answer this way: *'If you take two shillings as your share and another man wants 2s. 6d. kill him. Similarly, if a man accepts 2s. while you have 2s. 6d., kill*

---

[1] *Do We Agree?*
[2] Ibid.
[3] Ibid.

163

him....' He now proposed to ask Mr Chesterton *'Do you agree with that?'*

Chesterton came to his feet with an emphatic—No. *'He does not really think any more than I do, that all the people in this hall, who have already created some confusion, should increase the confusion by killing each other and searching each other's pockets'* in order to distinguish the two shilling people from the half-crown. But he wanted to turn to more important things. He had heard from the lips of all Socialists the phrase which *'Mr Shaw has with characteristic artfulness avoided . . . "that the means of production should be owned by the community".'* [Here he paused, fumbled with an old envelope which resembled his notes, adjusted his pince-nez at a still more crooked angle, threw down the envelope and ploughed on.] He did not like the word 'community'. He preferred the word 'Commons' and he would say this in agreement with Shaw—that the Commons should certainly own the means of production.

Beyond that, divergence was violent. *'It is not my fault if [Mr Shaw] has remained young, while I have grown in comparison wrinkled and haggard, old and experienced and acquainted with the elementary facts of life. . . .'* But clearly when the *State* took over the means of production the *Commons*—or the ordinary people—lost it. Even if all the citizens had an equal share of State income they would still have no control whatever over the proper disposal of the capital.

'I begin at the other end. . . . Let us so far as is possible in the complicated affairs of humanity, put into the hands of the Commons the control of its means of production—and real control. The man who owns a piece of land controls it in a direct . . . sense.' So it was with owning a piece of machinery, tools or even a workshop. *'But if you establish, right in the middle of the State, one enormous machine, if you turn the handle of that machine, and somebody, who must be an official . . . distributes'* the proceeds, the Commons have lost ownership, control, direction, everything. The danger of tyrannous abuse of centralized control was axiomatic. Any group

could be singled out and obliterated for anti-social tendencies or even less.

Mr Shaw, Chesterton concluded, had made a great to-do about the redistribution of wealth, and clearly there was a lot in this; but what they, the Distributists, wanted to do was something much more fundamental—to redistribute power.

Shaw now gave a swift piece of economic analysis probably incomprehensible to many in the audience since it was, in the rush of wit, laughter and the urge to deal with more clear-cut problems, left with very ragged ends. When he said, '*We must be perfectly clear as to what capital is*' and answered '*capital is spare money*', he knew he could not leave it like that; but his illustration of the man who had more of the means of subsistence than he could use and spent it to employ another man, was not very illuminating.

Shaw continued: '*Mr Chesterton has formed the Distributist League which organized this meeting. . . . What was the very first thing this League said, must be done? It said that the coal mines should be nationalized.*' Instead of insisting that the miners' means of production should be made his own property, or that he should have control over it, the League was '*forced to advocate making national property of the coal mines*', a move indistinguishable from Socialism. It knew, in the first place, that if you ask the man working in the mine to manage the mine he answered '*Not me . . . that's your job*'. But it did not know something else which Shaw must make very clear. When nationalized, these mines would not be managed by the House of Commons. . . . '*Under the present capitalistic system [the owner] has to surrender [control] to the manager. . . . Under Socialism he would have to surrender [control] to the manager appointed by the Coal Master General. That would not prevent the product of the mine being equally distributed among the people.*' Blandly and without pausing for any comment from Chesterton, Shaw pressed on. '*Now that Mr Chesterton agrees that the coal mines will have to be nationalized he will be led by the same pressure of facts to agree to the nationalization of everything else. . . .*' [Laughter.]

There was a murderously mistaken correlation between power and property. Under capitalism, which could not possibly be tolerated in a society pretending to be civilized, a landlord could throw people off his land whenever he chose, '*or take a woman in child-bearing and eject her into the snow and leave her there*'. Oh no—it was no use protesting that the Old Exaggerator was at the game again. These things had, unquestionably, been done.

Compare such unbridled powers with the powers he had over a piece of his, Shaw's, own property—his umbrella—which belonging as it did to his wife, he would temporarily confiscate. '*I have a very limited legal right to the use of this umbrella. I cannot do as I like with it. For instance certain passages in Mr Chesterton's speech tempted me to get up and smite him over the head with my umbrella. . . .*' But if he did this he would '*soon be made aware, possibly by Mr Belloc's fist—that I cannot treat my umbrella as my own property in the way in which a landlord treats his land*'.[1]

Shaw was not one of these lack-lustre lackeys of Socialism wanting to take the sparkle out of life; he merely wanted '*to destroy ownership in order that possession and enjoyment*' might '*be raised to the highest point in every section of the community. . . .*'

Chesterton answered: '*Among the bewildering welter of fallacies which Mr Shaw has just given us I prefer to deal first with the simplest. When Mr Shaw refrains from hitting me over the head with his umbrella, the real reason*' . . . is that he happens '*not to own my head. . . .*' [Laughter.][2]

Of course coal was an exception. Of course the Distributists were sane enough to see that certain things had to be taken over by the State, but their number was strictly limited. No one wanted personally owned and designed postage stamps subjectively affixed to hand-made envelopes. As for this stuff of Shaw's about the miner not wanting to run the mines, it certainly wasn't true of the peasant. '*I cannot agree . . . that peasants do not*

[1] *Do We Agree?*
[2] Ibid.

like peasant property because I know the reverse . . .' to be true. There was a great deal more in the same manner, which once again built an effective counter case.

Then it was Shaw's turn again and he at once asked: Why does Chesterton insist that *'coal mines are an exception? Are they an exception?'* Without waiting for an answer he ploughed on: The fundamental reason why they must nationalize the coal mines lay in the fantastic inequality of production costs between one mine and another. In Sunderland you could pick up coal in a perambulator and the cost was very low, in Whitehaven tunnels had to be driven into the sea bed and the cost was very high. *'The reason why you have to pay such monstrous prices for your coal is that they are fixed by the cost of making submarine mines. . . . Everyone can see at once that in order to have any kind of equable dealing in coal,'* you must *'charge the citizens the average cost for the total national supply'*—which meant nationalization.

This brought him to the real crux. Coal was no fanciful Socialist exception—it was the general rule. It applied with rather more force where land worth the price of a maharajah's ransom per acre in one place, was within half an hour by taxi ride from land worth rather less than Mr Chesterton's opinions on coal. *'Mr Chesterton in arriving at the necessity for the nationalization of the coal mines has started on his journey towards the nationalization of all industries. If he goes on to the land and from the land to the factory and from there to every other industrial department, he will find that every successive case is an exception. . . .'*

As to the profound instinct for property which Mr Chesterton imagined to be implanted by the divinity in such a variety of types, including peasants—it might exist in the country but not in the towns. *'People are content to live in houses they do not own: when they possess them they often find them a great nuisance.'* In any case he, Shaw, could easily persuade people to give up this instinct to private property. Fundamentally the means of production and therefore the wealth in any country were the men and women themselves.

M   167

Chesterton replied: '*We are trying to deal with human beings, creatures quite outside the purview of Mr Shaw and his political philosophy. We know town people are . . . different from country people. . . . We know man's irrepressible desire to own property and because some landlords have been cruel, it is no use talking of abolishing, denying, and destroying property. . . .*'

All this was so appallingly characteristic of Shaw. He represented a morality of negations. When he said that he could persuade all men to give up the sentiment of private property, it was in exactly the same spirit that he believed tobacco, meat and beer could be abandoned. To him, Chesterton, it was not only a chilly prospect; it was a serious intervention with the laws of nature.

Again he developed his case elaborately and at last he concluded: '*Mr Shaw said . . . that men and women are the only means of production*', and he was driven back to the old Socialist phrase —the ownership of the means of production. '*I quite accept the parallel. His proposition is that the government, the officials, of the State, should own the men and women, in other words that the men and women should become slaves. . . .*' It really was the most preposterous and dangerous nonsense.

So it went on. Not merely for this brief debate, but for years. They agreed to differ in the most prolonged and eloquent way.

If there were those who believed that neither could have very deep convictions and remain on such good terms, they overlooked not merely the common humanity of both, but their ability to convince one another of this deeper identity. If there were those who suspected that the whole thing was rigged, that two theatrically minded authors had duped their audiences for the sake of sheer display, this was far removed from the civilized ideals both sought to serve.

They were to continue in touch for some years. They were to write and meet occasionally until that day when Chesterton's heart began to fail him and presently his friends grew worried. Their regard for one another remained until the beautiful

June day when Shaw wrote his last letter to Mrs Chesterton, a letter which Chesterton could no longer read.

But that was not yet. Ten more years were to elapse. Meanwhile another battle had to be fought.

CHAPTER SIX

Hilaire Belloc versus H. G. Wells

LATE IN 1925 and early 1926 a revised and illustrated version of H. G. Wells' *Outline of History* was published in fortnightly parts. As each part appeared Hilaire Belloc launched lengthy attacks upon it in the Catholic *Universe*. According to Wells *'they were grossly personal and provocative in tone, and no doubt a great joy and comfort to the faithful'*.[1] Unrestrained by Chesterton's good nature, once more the willing victim of a great gift for rage, Wells burst his banks and poured out six articles, only to find that no one outside the Catholic world had heard of Belloc's articles and none of Fleet Street's irreligious editors was prepared to bore his audience with a dispute towards which they felt a quite pagan indifference. Whereupon Wells slapped all six articles in to the editor of the Catholic *Universe* and offered for publication free of charge what was probably worth £600. The *Universe* remained unmoved. It did not, even gratis, want to contaminate its columns with Mr Wells. Wells dictated a letter.

'*My dear Sir,*

'*I am sorry to receive your letter of May 19. May I point out to you that Mr Belloc has been attacking my reputation as a thinker, a writer, an impartial historian and an educated person for four and twenty fortnights in the* Universe? *He has misquoted; he has mis-stated. Will your Catholic public tolerate no reply?*'

The editor of the *Universe* went into consultation with the directors and Hilaire Belloc. A whole month's examination at last produced an offer to Mr Wells to correct any point of fact where he might have been misrepresented. '*Disinclined for a series of wrangles upon what might and might not be a "point of fact"* '

[1] *Mr Belloc Objects*, p.v. 1926. H. G. Wells.

the indefatigable Wells sprang into another book, alive with retaliation and splendidly invoking all his scientific gods.

The articles which provoked this book were certainly stimulating, personal and full of destructive irony. Each carried highly subjective titles: *Mr Wells and The Creation of Man—Mr
Wells and the Fall of Man—Mr Wells and God*. The series opened
with a number of tributes to Wells' powers of writing, his sincerity and lucidity, to be followed by asides about his origins,
scholarship and limitations. Then came what Belloc regarded as
'four crushing a priori' arguments against the natural selection so
elaborately propounded by Wells.

He commented on Wells' knowledge of pre-history: *'He does
not . . . remark that the original guess at the cranial capacity of the
Piltdown Man was too small, certainly by 30 per cent and possibly 50
per cent. He does not tell his readers the remarkably high angle of the
forehead, nor the really disturbing fact that there appear to have been
no strong orbital ridges. And why are his readers not given all this?
Because—like so many facts in Pre-history—they interfere with the
simple "progress" idea and would make the reader understand how
very little we do know about early man and his ancestry, and what an
intolerable amount of theory there is to a halfpenny worth of fact. For
the Piltdown Man, on all the orthodox hypotheses, has got to be enormously older than Neanderthal Man—and yet has a much more
modern brain-box.'*[1]

Belloc said he found so much of Mr Wells' pretentious nonsense hopelessly dated. As he read Wells on the Evolution of the
Idea of God, he recalled cataracts of similar stuff from Grant
Allen to Max Muller. He was back in his youth, *'back in the days
of the Bustle and the Bang, of Knowles' Nineteenth Century, of
Sweetness and Light and many another faded picture and phrase that
turn me cold with the mere memory of them . . . I smell the gas of the
old gas-burners, and I hear the wheels of the hansom cab along the
London streets and the clatter of horse hoofs in Pall Mall. . . .'*[2]

---

[1] *A Companion to Mr Wells' Outline of History*, p. 30, Hilaire Belloc.
[2] Ibid., p. 36.

Mr Wells was a pastmaster at bringing out these *'venerable contraptions'*, he said. Look at this Old Man theory for instance. According to Wells and many others, when Man was still at a bestial stage of development, he went about in groups consisting of *'a father, several mothers and a lot of young'*. The group lived in terror of the Father and as the young males matured and showed signs of interest in other females, the Old Man turned his full ferocity upon them and drove them out of the group into the wilderness. Sometimes the sons rebelled, murdered the father and divided the women amongst them. In due time, stories passed from mother to daughter and son, and the exploits of the Old Man became obsessional to the point where he developed quasi-supernatural characteristics eventually giving man his first idea of God. *'. . . what I would like to point out,'* Belloc commented, *'is not so much the offensiveness of the picture . . . as its gratuitous inanity. . . . It is one thing to confuse hypothesis with fact—and bad enough, God knows—but it is a still more degraded thing for the human intelligence to descend to mere unsupported affirmation. . . .*

'Let us get this point quite clear—for it applies to the whole of Mr Wells' work. Not only is hypothesis stated as fact, but things are stated as fact which aren't even hypothesis—which have no evidence at all in their favour. . . .'[1]

Belloc believed that there was absolutely no trace of a vertebrate ancestral to man possessing the habits described by Wells. The whole story was invented from beginning to end. Wells had done no more than copy it out of other people's old books. He had far better, for the sake of his reputation, have left it alone. *'It looks silly enough today, and in a few years' time it will look far sillier.'*[2]

Wells was so conveniently inconsistent. Having traced religion to *'certain past terrors and offensive habits in a bestial type prior to Man'*, he *'won't allow it in palaeolithic man long after'*, and *'then*

[1] *A Companion to Mr Wells' Outline of History*, p. 37. Hilaire Belloc.
[2] Ibid.

he suddenly recurs to it in neolithic man far later still. How familiar it all is![1] Belloc exclaimed.

He continued in this vein for 114 large pages, raking every aspect of Wells' book with ingenious crossfire from the Creation, the Fall of Man and Buddhism, to the Incarnation and the Origins of the Church. Particularly he gave careful attention to Wells and Darwin, Wells and Natural Selection, Wells and his nonsense about the embryo climbing up the family tree. He questioned Wells' history and authorities, invoking Vialleton and scores of European authorities to support his own case, spreading lavishly into an appendix. Wells' book, he concluded, *'will have a vast circulation . . . and an early grave'*. It was all, on Belloc's part, a considerable performance for a man primarily a literary man.

Wells' reply opened with what must be *the* classic underestimate of the greatest literary fighter of the early twentieth century—*'I am the least controversial of men'*, and then followed the astounding statement that *'I bring an unskilled pen to the task'*.[2]

Whether H.G. hoped to disarm any Catholic reader, or whether his remarkable powers of stepping into one incarnation after another, led him to attempt the most difficult metamorphosis of all—Wells the modest—he could not sustain the role for long.

Certainly the first two pages were restrained. Of course he claimed that he was *'conscious of no animus against Catholicism'* when he seemed to recoil from it as the devil from holy water: and he repeated that he accepted *'the gospels as historical documents of primary value'* defended Christianity against Gibbon and acknowledged the *'role of the Church in preserving learning in Europe, consolidating Christendom, and extending knowledge from a small developed class to the whole community'*.[3]

[1] *A Companion to Mr Wells' Outline of History*, p. 37. Hilaire Belloc.
[2] *Mr Belloc Objects*, p. 1. H. G. Wells.
[3] Ibid.

What really interested him at the outset was Mr Belloc's new pose. '*Accustomed as I am to see Mr Belloc dodging about in my London club . . . and even occasionally appearing at a dinner party, compactly stout, rather breathless and always insistently garrulous, I am more than a little amazed at his opening. He has suddenly become aloof from me. A great gulf of manners yawns between us. "Hullo Belloc!" is frozen on my lips. . . . He advances upon me in his Introduction with a gravity of utterance, a dignity of gesture, rare in God-fearing, sober men.*'[1]

Belloc had described Wells as sincere, honest and a patriot, with intentions only to be described as worthy, but the note quickly changed, Wells said. He, Wells, became in no time an Englishman of the Home Counties and London Suburbs, who knew nothing of any language, science or literature outside England; a suburban Mr Wells unaware that '*foreigners*' had '*general histories*'. The shrinking process, Wells said, continued with the collapse of the Royal College of Science into a mere mechanics' institute and the revelation that this low class fellow had an appalling prejudice against the gentry of his own country. A profound and incurable illiteracy in certain fields followed '*as a matter of course*'.

Far worse, this new Wells did not really believe '*from the bottom of his heart all that he read in the text-books of his youth*'. He had copied things from the wrong books. '*One can see that base malignant . . . fellow*' (Wells wrote) '*in his stuffy room all hung with Union Jacks, with the "wrong", the "Protestant" book flattened out before him, copying, copying. . . .*'

What exactly was Belloc trying to do? Why did he first praise, then blame and then abuse so second rate a popular idol as he made Wells out to be? Psychologists might be interested by the phenomenon of the giant Belloc bothering with this gnat; historians might wonder why he troubled to expose a fellow self-condemned by his own superficialities; scientists of the same calibre as Belloc must regret the wasting of such skills and

[1] *Mr Belloc Objects*, p. 2. H. G. Wells.

scholarship on so worthless a target; but he, Wells, knew what was hidden behind all this.

'*I realized long ago that his apparent arrogance is largely the self-protection of a fundamentally fearful man. He is a stout fellow in a funk. He is the sort of man who talks loud and fast for fear of hearing the other side. There is a frightened thing at the heart of all this burly insolence. . . .*'

Perhaps it would be as well to come down to earth and recapitulate the theory of natural selection as represented by real authorities. It was very necessary to do this because Belloc had got the whole thing '*suitably askew*'. He was muddle-headed. He did not quote, Wells said, he paraphrased, in the process putting certain words between inverted commas . . . '*so as inadvertently to produce the impression that they are mine. . . .*'

Belloc appeared to believe that certain scientists set out with the presupposition that it would be a good thing to get rid of God and eventually pieced together enough evidence to satisfy the most atheistical, which resulted in the theory of Natural Selection. He seemed unaware that years of research had preceded the formulation of this theory and did not remotely understand how 70 years of careful checking, of ransacking the whole range of vital phenomena had only made the theory, with minor adjustments, more secure.

Here, then, was the recapitulation. Every individual organism in every species had its own differences, and those differences which were advantageous gave it higher chances of survival. '*Therefore, taking a species as a whole by the million or billion or million billion . . . there will be in each successive generation a greater number of individuals with the differences that are advantageous, relative to the number with disadvantages.*' In other words, the average of the species will have moved more or less in the direction of the advantageous differences, whatever they may be, and however numerous they may be.

Belloc talked glibly of the embryo climbing up the family tree, putting those words into inverted commas as though he,

Wells, had used them. ' . . . *it is only by straining my charity to the utmost that I can accept that this was an accident.*' Of course there was a tendency for certain embryos to '*recapitulate*' earlier stages in their evolution, but any modern text book of embryology made it quite clear that '*the life cycle can be and is modified at any point, and that an embryo has much more serious work in hand than reciting its family history*'.

Belloc had written: '*He [Mr Wells] doesn't know that Vailleton of Montpellier has knocked the last nail into the coffin of that facile and superficial Victorian short-cut . . . [the family tree]. He has probably never heard of Vailleton and when he does he will suspect him for a foreigner. That is what I mean by being provincial and not abreast of one's time. . . .*'

Quite true, Wells said. He had '*never heard of any Vailleton in biological science*'. But it was possible that the hasty Mr Belloc had in mind '*that eminent Victorian embryologist, Vialleton, who, so far from being the very newest thing in "European biology", must now be getting on for 70*'. Vialleton derived from Haeckel who invented the family tree idea and Vialleton was still poised half-way back down that particular line of theoretical development. Conceivably, years ago, certain French students had '*run away with the idea that embryos consciously repeat their phylogeny. . . . It is not an idea I have ever entertained . . . its only interest here is that it gives Mr Belloc a chance of showing how rudely he can set out his inaccuracies. . . .*'[1]

Belloc came back with a total disclaimer of any pretensions on his part to '*being a man having special learning with European reputation in such affairs*'. All this stuff of Wells' was the '*mere explosion of a man in a passion*'. If the capacity to make an opponent foam—and foam unnecessarily—at the mouth was any test of winning an argument, then he had clearly won hands down, for Wells could not even see a series of simple compliments straightforwardly. Belloc had said that Wells was sincere, wrote lucidly, was accurate in detailed references, and where another

[1] *Mr Belloc Objects*, p. 21. H. G. Wells.

man might graciously accept such praise, he simply fell into a rage. All this became a strange condition of '*oiliness*' in the written word of Hilaire Belloc. As for the eminent Victorian embryologist. . . . Anyone familiar with biological history would have known that V*a*illeton was a slip for V*ia*lleton but Wells had to write a whole page about it, ironically assuming that they were two different people in order to win a cheap debating point out of all proportion to a microscopic error.

And then this so-called '*muddle-headedness*' of Belloc's. What could be more '*muddle-headed than mixing up the general theory of evolution with the particular (and now moribund) materialist theory of Natural Selection*'. That was what Mr Wells perpetually did. It was possible to say that a man had travelled from London to Birmingham, but the theory of Natural Selection said that he '*travelled by motor car and not by railway*'. Mr Wells didn't seem to know the difference. '*The only issue in the controversy which Mr Wells has both misunderstood and rashly engaged in, is upon the agency of Evolution, not upon Evolution itself. Yet he has confused the two!*'[1]

It is difficult to know precisely when Wells wrote the different sections of his attacks on Belloc, but between the years 1923–5 symptoms of a self which constantly troubled him became more urgent. It was a self richly endowed with the fugitive impulse, a condition he had come to see as inseparable from the intellectual life. There were times in his life when he suddenly felt that he had to '*get away from all this and think . . . and begin again*'. Daily routines wrapped around him, embedding him in '*a mass of trite and habitual responses . . .*' and . . . '*I must have the refreshment of new sights, sounds, colours or I shall die away. . . .*'

It led him into bursts of restless irrationality. He would waste his own and his secretary's time writing long letters about the placing of an electric plug, complaining of the imbecility of electricians who should have known by instinct where Mr Wells required his plugs to go. Or he would plunge into a fresh

[1] *Mr Belloc Still Objects*, pp. 10–11. Hilaire Belloc.

and ferocious controversy. Or he would send his secretary packing into the park on a beautiful summer day, while he lay back on the sofa brooding over his next book—only to burst out again, ten minutes later, '*I must get away. I must forget all this—find new sights, sounds, colours. . . .*'

On this occasion he found them in the South of France. There, among the sunlit terraces, the orange trees, the olive groves and the flowers, he began to write that extraordinary bundle of fiction, argument and Wellsian soliloquy which came to be known as *The World of William Clissold*, and occasionally fell into fresh rages at the '*idiocies*' of Belloc.

Belloc, too, was a man now subject to deep depressions. Constantly slipping abroad for a few days, he diverted rage from everyday reality into his quarrels, and was quite as restless as Wells. To be found at lunch in the Gourmet with A. D. Peters and J. B. Morton he miraculously corrected proofs, made conversation, waited for a telephone call and somehow snatched food, all at once. '*What a life I lead*' he would say as he dashed down a note of something he must say to that intolerable little man Wells. And if the waiter took his time bringing the food '*It's impossible! We can't go on like this!*'[1] He could, on occasion, be quite choleric.

From lunch he hurried round to the Reform Club, or went to Bell Yard to dictate, or slipped in amongst the browsing forms at the London Library, anxious not to be waylaid and somehow giving the impression of a darkly conspiratorial figure hopelessly failing to render the magnificent frame anonymous. A drink before dinner at the Carlton Bar with J. B. Morton; dinner ran more easily with proofs receiving little attention: sometimes he sat on late; sometimes he went back early to his room in Church Street, Kensington, which he called his *bounge*. There he often slept badly and was up early to hear Mass in the church next door. At week-ends he frequently went down to Kings' Land, but it remained a mystery where he found time to

[1] *Hilaire Belloc*, p. 70. J. B. Morton.

continue pouring out books—another volume of the *History of England*, *Economics for Helen*, *The Cruise of the Nona*—and still managed to meet and return blow for blow from Wells. He was four years younger, he was twice—or was it three times— the size, he had a voice which could drown H.G.'s when raised, and he did not dissipate quite so much energy in what he some- times referred to, with lifted eyebrows, as Wells' '*emotioniala*'. Both men had torrential nervous energy, both could be savage- ly tenacious, both were freshly enraged by each new statement of the other, scorn in Wells sometimes accompanied, as he wrote his replies, by that high pitched chortling which occa- sionally went with the genius-boy. . . .

'*He* [Belloc] *produces . . . certain remarkable* a priori *arguments*', he wrote. '*The first is beautifully absurd. It is difficult to believe it is advanced in anything but a spirit of burlesque . . . He says that an advantage is not an advantage. He says that an advantage does not give an advantage unless it is combined with other advantages. You will think I am misrepresenting him . . . .*'

Not a bit of it. Just look at this quotation from Belloc, Wells said: '*The advantageous differences making for survival are not of one kind in any particular case, but of an indefinitely large number (e.g. climate getting colder needs not only warmer coat, but power to digest new food, protective colouring so as not to show dark against the snow, etc., an indefinitely large number of qualities). Now the chance of all being combined (and co-ordinated) in a single individual, without design, accidentally, let alone of their thus appearing in many individuals accidentally and without design, approximates to zero.*'

Belloc carried these statements to a logical conclusion which Wells understood to mean '*that only an individual possessing all the possible differences that are advantageous at any particular time can survive*'. What absolute, unmitigated nonsense it all was, Wells said . . . '*They may be advantages, but not sufficient advan- tages to score an advantage.*' Wells knew this sounded tipsy, but there it was in black and white. What it meant in effect was so outrageous that no one but a biological illiterate like Mr Belloc could have conceived such a statement. For it meant that, excepting a miracle, *'every species must be exterminated in every generation'*. Wells could see no other way out of such a postulate. And this was Mr Belloc's unfailing logic, his *'lucid Latin mind shining above my Nordic fog'*.

Of course it was possible Mr Belloc meant something else. If he had thought a little more, instead of muddling through, he might have arrived at a different statement and at the risk of offending him by helping him to think more clearly, he, Wells, would say it: There was some reason to assume that when a species came *'under stress of changing conditions'*, it was *'usual for the need for adaptation to be felt upon a number of points and not simply upon one, and that* since every advantage [my romans] *counts, the individual with the greatest combination of advantageous differences'* had *'the best chances'*. That did not in any way alter the very simple fact that a single advantage remained, whatever happened a single advantage.

Wells rushed on to isolate yet another quotation from Belloc which had to be read—he thought—to be believed, into such pseudo-scientific confusions did it fall. Belloc had taken the example of a reptile, originally wingless, but provided with some form of armour, and asked what happened in the interval between its ceasing to be strictly a reptile and becoming a bird. So far as he [Belloc] could follow the maunderings of certain biologists, Natural Selection set out to transform the legs of the reptile into wings, and the scales of the armour into feathers. As he understood it this was done by *'making the leg less and less of a leg for countless ages, and by infinite minute gradations, gradually turning the scales into feathers'*.

Could anything be more abysmally absurd, Belloc said. *'By the very nature of the theory'* if *'each stage in all these millions is an advantage over the last towards survival . . .'* what happens at the half-way stage? *'Compare the "get away" chances of a lizard at one end of the process or a sparrow at the other, with some poor beast that had to try to scurry off on half-wings or to fly with half-legs!'*

There was only one way of reconciling this preposterous nonsense with commonsense and that was by postulating a Design. Accept evolution as an experimental process instinct with ultimate design and it made sense. Without it, the whole thing collapsed.

Wells threw up his hands in a mixture of horror and delight. It was said that before he settled down to answer this piece of '*ingenious idiocy*' as part of a long sustained reply, he performed a caper round his writing desk, his small feet twinkling in the likeness of a dance.

Note, he wrote, '*a few of the things of which Mr Belloc shows himself . . . unaware in this amusing display of perplexity*'. He did not know that '*Mesozoic reptiles most closely resembling birds were creatures walking on their hind legs, with a bony structure of the loins and a backbone already suggestive of the avian anatomy. Nor is he aware that in the lowliest of living birds the fore-limbs are mere flappers, that the feathers are simpler in structure than any other birds' feathers, and that the general development of a bird's feathers points plainly to the elongation of a scale.*' Poor Belloc, he continued, had never picked up the elementary bit of information that feathers came before wings, and that at first they were not concerned with flying but '*with protection against cold*'. It was all in the *Outline of History* but Belloc had overlooked the relevant parts of that book. '*The transition from a quilled to a feathered dinosaur presents . . . no imaginative difficulties, and the earliest birds ran and did not fly.*' Amongst the earliest known extinct birds was the Hesperornis, a diving bird quite without wings. One complete category of living birds, including the ostrich and the emu, had no trace '*in their structure of any ancestral flying phase: their breast-bones are incapable of carrying the necessary muscular attachments*'.[1]

Once the feather was fully developed '*it opened up great possibilities of a strong and light extension of the flapper, helpful in running or useful in leaps from tree to tree*'. And the early bird Archoeopteryx, which appeared in the *Outline*, had '*a sort of bat-wing*

[1] *Mr Belloc Objects*, p. 26. H. G. Wells.

fore-limb with feathers instead of membrane. It was a woodland crea-ture, and flew as a flying fox or a flying lemur or even a bat flies . . .'[1]

It was Wells' opinion that these facts safely disposed of all the half-leg, half-wing troubles and made an awful '*hash*' of Belloc's argument. '*. . . how pitifully it scurries off before them on its nonde-script stumps of pretentious half-knowledge, half-impudence!*'

Wells' attack did not greatly bother Belloc. He stuck vigor-ously to his point. The elaborate co-ordination needed in thou-sands of special relations within complex animal organisms could not occur, together, by accident. Mr Wells imagined that he was merely attacking Hilaire Belloc as though these argu-ments were produced out of his own head. In fact it was part of the thinking of no less a person than Wolff . . . . '*It is clear that Mr Wells has never heard of Wolff; yet it is, I believe . . . nearly eighteen years since Wolff brought out this argument . . . .*' Here was the relevant quotation:

He, Wolff, could '*imagine a gradual development of the adapta-tion between one muscle-cell and one nerve-ending, through selection among an infinity of chance-made variations; but that such shall take place coincidently in time and character in hundreds of thousands of cases in one organism is inconceivable*'.

Mr Wells not Mr Belloc had become confused over the transformation of the legs into wings. Belloc's argument wasn't in the least disturbed by the existence of intermediate forms; if one could prove the transformation—which one could not— what on earth would it have to do with Natural Selection? '*It would be*', Belloc continued, '*simply an example of transformism*', without giving any very precise definition of what he meant by the word.

Then came the same point massively reiterated with even greater conviction. '*What I say . . . is that between the foot of the land animal and the flapper of the whale, between the powerfully defensive and aggressive great ape, and the weak, more intelligent man, there must be stages (if the transition ever took place) where the*

[1] *Mr Belloc Objects*, p. 26. H. G. Wells.

organism was at a positive disadvantage, and that consideration blows Darwinian Natural Selection to pieces. . . .'[1]

If Wells and Belloc seemed deep enough in the biological jungle to satisfy the most casuistical, what Wells called '*the final of a "wonderful trinity of a prioris"'* still needed attention. This was the theory once put forward by Lord Salisbury at the British Association. It said that if only a limited number of individuals had all the survival value differences in the correct proportion amongst millions who had not, how did they ever come together to breed and perpetuate their advantages?

Mr Belloc, Wells said, was driven once again to fall back upon that remarkable process he called Design. He '*makes his Creative Spirit, which has already urged these two individuals, lions or liver flukes . . . or what not, to make an effort and adapt themselves, lead them . . . to their romantic and beneficial nuptials, while the theory of Natural Selection grinds its teeth in the background . . . .'*

Mr Belloc's fundamental trouble was that he had 'got the whole business upside down'—in dictation Wells was said to have used the blunter equivalent. He did not entirely blame Belloc for this, but rather the early Darwinians who had misled many people by using the phrase 'Survival of the Fittest'. Mr Belloc might have some excuse for being misled himself if he did not pretend to have read Mr Wells' *Outline of History*, but page 16 of that 'modest compendium' clearly stated that it was much more accurate to speak of the Survival of the Fitter, and whatever pretensions Mr Belloc had to an alibi disappeared. Evolution should not be seen in terms of individuals but of species. '*Yet Mr Belloc insists upon writing of "the Fittest" as a sort of conspicuously competitive prize boy, a favourable "sport", who has to meet his female equivalent and breed a new variety. . . .'*

Wells didn't know whether Belloc's mathematical attainments were high, but if he was able to understand what an average meant, he had to face up to the fact that the '*characteristics of a species are determined by its average specimens. This*

[1] *Mr Belloc Still Objects*, p. 20. Hilaire Belloc.

dickering about with fancy stories of abnormal nuptials has nothing to do with the theory of Natural Selection.'

In order not to misrepresent Belloc it would be as well at this point to develop in more detail the glittering names he summoned to his aid. Really Mr Wells flattered him too much, he said. His assumption that he, Belloc, was solely responsible for all these arguments was pleasing but quite untrue. Perhaps Mr Wells might not so lightly dismiss them if he realized what a weight of professional authority was massed behind them, but it must be very difficult for Mr Wells to take account of authorities he had probably never read. To begin with there was a person called Professor Bateson who said: '*We*' (biologists in general) '*have come to the conviction that the principle of Natural Selection cannot have been the chief factor in determining species.'* Wells would automatically ask with contempt—Who is this man Bateson? None other than the President of the British Association when it met in Melbourne in 1914. Similarly a name like Driesch could only excite open scorn from Mr Wells. Quite patently he had never heard of him. He had, in fact, never heard of half the people and things inconvenient to his theory. But it so happened that Driesch was among the '*greatest of the German biologists*' . . . and had proclaimed: '*For men of clear intellect, Darwinism had long been dead. . . .'*

An American named Dwight put the same point far more emphatically: '*We have now the remarkable spectacle that just when many scientific men are all agreed that there is* no part (Belloc's romans) *of the Darwinian system that is of any great influence, and that as a whole the theory is not only unproved, but impossible, the ignorant, half-educated masses have acquired the idea that it is to be accepted as a fundamental fact. . . .'*

And who, Wells would tirelessly reiterate—who in the devil is this fellow Dwight? Why, no less than Professor of Anatomy at Harvard University in the United States of America.

Wells had recklessly asserted that Belloc's authorities did not exist, but he could go on quoting them until Mr Wells was deafened by their names. Unfortunately it would make no difference. Mr Wells was deaf already.

H. G. did not deign to deal with his alleged deafness. He was, he said, more interested in another statement of Belloc's. In this statement he suddenly demanded a continuous '*series of changing forms passing one into the other*' from the geological record; not merely a convincing number of intermediate forms but the whole linked chain of grandfather, father and son. '*He does not say whether he insists upon a pedigree with the bones and proper certificates of birth, but I suppose it comes down to that.* . . . ' Of course it was highly reprehensible of the lower animals to bury their dead without properly dating their remains in the first place, but such he feared was the case. It left Wells with nothing more than '*an extraordinary display of fossil types*' in camels, horses and elephants '*exhibiting step by step the development and differentiation of species and genera.* . . .'

There was one complication in conceding Mr Belloc his point. Unfortunately he did not understand the way in which the rocks left a record of early history. He did not understand that when the bed of an estuary gradually sank it might give place to marine sands, or fresh water might carry down gravels which overlaid the original shingle. '*Now if he will think what would happen today under such circumstances, he will realize that the fauna and flora of the stratum first considered will drift away, and that another fauna and flora will come in with the new conditions. Fresh things will come to feed and wade and drown in the waters, and old types will no longer frequent them. The fossil remains of one stratum are very rarely directly successive to those below it or directly ancestral to those above it.*' A succession of forms was therefore much more difficult to follow than Mr Belloc, with his over simplified pictures, would ever know.

More important still, the chances of the bones of a rabbit finding a resting place where they could safely fossilize and await the geologists' investigations were not very high in proportion to the millions of rabbits whose bones simply disintegrated in dust. Taken against a background of millions of years it was childish of Mr Belloc to expect '*an unbroken series of forms*'.

Sometime before Belloc published *Mr Belloc Still Objects*, in 1926, Wells was said to have made a flying visit from the South of France to London and in the Reform Club they met by accident. Wells was fumbling under his chair for a dropped box of matches when Belloc, passing through the smoking room, paused a few feet from him and murmured '*Still looking for Neanderthal Man, H.G.?*' And Wells, bobbing up a pink face, instantly retorted '*No—Woman.*' Whereupon Belloc passed silently on.

The story was probably apocryphal and meant nothing beyond suggesting a camaraderie which did not in fact any longer exist.

More accurate were the bare bones of another encounter hinted at by Robert Speaight in his *Life of Hilaire Belloc*. '*Wells, for all his faults, was a man of warm affections and he could not understand how Belloc could attack him so violently and yet bear him no personal ill will. He was bitterly resentful and there was a painful scene at the Reform Club. . . .*'[1]

Both men were now considerably disillusioned with life, both had brought tremendous courage to facing their respective difficulties. Belloc was used to crusading on behalf of minorities but the resilience with which he rose from his anti-Dreyfusard, Pro-Boer and pro-Catholic battles as a young man had slackened. Underneath his zest for living, his wit and humour, ran sad undercurrents and as Monsignor Knox now remarked '*his face never looked happy in repose*'. Caught off his guard his expression went beyond sadness into melancholy, but like Wells he could blaze up in a moment into laughter, anger, gaiety. Like Wells, too, he had immense sanity and vigour. He continued to be an aggressive talker, and Wells said that trying to talk to Belloc was like trying to break into a hail storm of one inch lumps. His friends put this down to force of character: Wells to vanity and pig-headedness.

[1] *The Life of Hilaire Belloc,* p. 402. Robert Speaight.

Wells' disillusion in the years 1925–8 had many roots. He was deeply involved with a brilliant but erratic woman who spoke a passionate English capable of stirring the dullest listener. Inevitably two such incandescent souls consumed one another and the depth and degree of their quarrels was in proportion to their talents.

In the fascinating welter of his quarrel with Belloc there were endless points which cannot satisfactorily be represented here. They became too technical.[1] In the end Belloc made his most powerful challenge on quite different grounds. But there remains one other point of detail which must be examined first. Belloc had quoted from page 55 of the *Outline of History* these words about palaeolithic man of the cave drawings: *'it is doubtful if they knew of the bow'*. When he first read this sentence, Belloc said that he was *'so staggered'* he could hardly believe he had read aright. *'That a person pretending to teach popular prehistorical science in 1925 should tell us of the cave painters that it was "doubtful if they knew of the bow" seemed to me quite of out nature.'*

'It was the more extraordinary because here before me, in Mr Wells' own book, were reproductions of these cave paintings, with the bow and the arrow appearing all over them . . . .' Clearly there was only one explanation of this appalling gaff on the part of a man like Wells; he was possessed with the necessity of making the facts fit his own fancy theology.

Wells came back. *'Palaeolithic man, speaking generally, was not an archer. Only the later Palaeolithic men, dealing with a smaller quarry than the reindeer, seem to have used the bow.'* It was not Wells who was fitting his facts in to some preconceived theology—as if he, Wells, had any theology—but Mr Belloc. *'He is inventing an error which is incredible even to himself as he invents*

[1] Anyone sufficiently interested to read the full record in accurate sequence should turn to three books: *A Companion to Mr Wells' Outline of History*, Hilaire Belloc; *Mr Belloc Objects*, H. G. Wells; and *Mr Belloc Still Objects*, Hilaire Belloc.

it and he is filling up space as hard as he can with indignation at my imaginary offence . . . .'

Belloc simply referred Wells back to his own words in the *Outline*. There, Belloc wrote, 'in the middle *of this description of later Palaeolithic Man (who, remember, had no bows and arrows) he has a set of paragraphs (on page 53) describing the well-known fact that these men executed drawings on rock surfaces. On the same page is given a specimen of these drawings, and above it, by way of title, the caption "Mural Painting by Palaeolithic Man". This mural painting is nothing else but bows and arrows!'*

Belloc proceeded to give other quotations which made confusion worse confounded. What—what on earth was he to make of it all—and indeed of Mr Wells? For his part he would not be surprised if Mr Wells *'had written his first section, putting an end to Palaeolithic Man and introducing Neolithic Man, before he had been told of the supposed later Palaeolithic Men, who had bows and arrows: that'* in fact *'he put in these latest Palaeolithic men as an afterthought'*.

At last came what Belloc regarded as a far more serious, and destructive argument against Wells. He was astonished that out of his prolonged examination of Wells' 'theories', an examination running to a hundred thousand words, Wells could, it seemed, find no more than six 'specific grievances of mis-statement'. Were the whole of the rest of Belloc's objections to remain untouched? All Wells could do about the greater part of Belloc's criticism was *'to fill a pamphlet with loud personal abuse'*.

In concluding phrases Wells made considerable play with Neanderthal Man. He had always wondered what Mr Belloc would say about Neanderthal Man. *'Would he put it before or after the Fall? Would he correct its anatomy by a wonderful new science out of his safe?'* Apparently not. Apparently Mr Belloc had nothing to say about Neanderthal Man. Nothing whatever. He set out with the preconceived idea that Man was a fixed type, using all the force of italics to drive it home, for the convenience of his own theology. Unfortunately *apart from Mr Belloc's assertion, there is no evidence that Man is any exception to the rest of living creatures. He changes. They all change.'* It was all an exercise in the niceties of belief: there was no attempt to demonstrate. *'Mr Belloc emerges where he went in, with much said and nothing proved, and the Outline undamaged by his attack.'* Wells suddenly found this quotation from Belloc: *'Sympathy or antagonism with the Catholic faith is the only thing of real importance in attempting to teach history.'* *'And there,'* said Wells triumphantly, *'you are! All these argumentations, gesticulations, all these tortured attempts to confute, are acts of devotion to Mr Belloc's peculiar vision of the Catholic faith.'*

One of Belloc's many last words—extending over several pages—was a jibe at the very special qualifications Wells appeared to have for talking about the Catholic faith. *'He tells us, rather pathetically, that he must know all about the Catholic Church, because he now winters on the Riviera . . . from what I have seen of those who thus escape the English winter, the Monte Carlo Express and the Cosmopolitan hotels do not make for common culture, let alone for an understanding of divine things. . . .'*

In two such skilled controversialists, convinced of each other's blind devotion to the wrong cause, it was not unexpected that each emerged, in his own eyes, triumphant.

The prolonged lull which followed was never, in any sustained sense, broken, so far as I can trace.

CHAPTER SEVEN

In the End

THE YEARS slipped away and one by one the antagonists. It seemed incredible that men with so much life, vigour and eloquence, with such painfully acquired skills and experience, could ever be brought low by anything short of suicide.

In 1936 the doctor thought very seriously of the state of G. K. Chesterton's heart. Presently, when too ill to be visited, Chesterton promised an unexpected visitor a poem on St Martin of Tours because '*he was a true Distributist*'.[1]

Not long afterwards Father Vincent arrived in response to a message from Chesterton's wife. Taken to the sick room he sang the Salve Regina over a man they now knew to be dying. In the full glory of a beautiful June day in 1936, people came from London, France and America to the funeral. Shaw was not there but on the following day he wrote to Mrs Frances Chesterton: '*It seems the most ridiculous thing in the world that I, eighteen years older than Gilbert, should be heartlessly surviving him. However, this is only to say that if you have any temporal bothers that I can remove, a line on a postcard (or three figures) will be sufficient. The trumpets are sounding for him; and the slightest interruption must be intolerable. Faithfully, G.B.S.*'

Belloc lived to be eighty-two. He was to fight magnificently against the encroachment of old age, singing lustily far into life, a rugged individualist indomitable until that moment when he fell near the fireplace and as the doctor examined his burns '*had a grand slanging match with him*'.[2]

Coulton—at last reduced to arguing with his family alone—grew frailer and more dependent on an ancient bath chair, but his decline was marked by the same courage and tenacity, the

[1] *Gilbert Keith Chesterton*, p. 551. Maisie Ward.
[2] *Hilaire Belloc*, p. 179. J. B. Morton.

same ruthless attention to detail which he had brought to his scholarship.

Shaw continued untroubled by reflections on the past, and the horizon, rapidly emptying of old friends and enemies, remained steady and clear to his ironical gaze. And Wells—Wells was very aware of the onset of old age, of the death of one friend after another, of the richly comic tragedy of his own declining body, with one whole lung and kidney left to breathe and live by, and diabetes, a weak heart and catarrh continuing to try the almost impossible task of killing him.

In 1936 literary London arranged a party to celebrate his 70th birthday and Somerset Maugham wrote:

'*Hundreds of people came to it. Bernard Shaw, a magnificent figure with his height, his white beard and white hair, his clear skin and bright eyes, made a speech. He stood very erect, his arms crossed, and with his puckish humour said many things highly embarrassing to the guest of the evening.*'[1] Wells buried his nose in his speech which he read from manuscript:

' "*It is a fine thing to be entertained by a great crowd of friends and I cannot tell you how much I enjoy being praised and having my importance so generously and delightfully exaggerated. I feel uplifted, expanded . . . . Yet all the same I will confess that the mellow brightness of this occasion is not without a shadow. I hate being seventy. To make this festival perfect you should have discovered that there had been some mistake and that I was forty-five. . . .*" '

H. G. Wells lived for another ten years. His health did not seriously break down until the last eighteen months and in his early seventies he continued active, eloquent, quite ready for any fresh antagonist, but presently half a dozen complications grew progressively worse.

In 1944 the doctors told him he could not last another year and their verdict did not so much dismay as anger him. Presently there were times when he sat in his sun trap at No. 13 Hanover Terrace, a panama hat jammed down on his head,

[1] *A Writer's Notebook.* Somerset Maugham.

listening to Mozart on his gramophone, an old man nodding in the half light of death. But when an unexpected visitor arrived during one of these recitals he immediately burst out with all his old vigour—'*Don't interrupt me—can't you see I'm dying?*' He grew terribly tired and irritable, irritable like a sick child, but sometimes out of the visibly shrinking husk, something resembling the old fire struck again.

There was no fuss in the way he finally died. On August 13, 1946, he sent the nurse out of the room. Ten minutes later she came in—and he was dead. Such a death as this there had not been since Dickens vanished from the European scene. Within a week Shaw had written his obituary:

'*So our H.G. is no more. He has written his own epitaph and his own biography, which is, like most autobiographies, much more candid than any second-hand account of him is likely to be . . . .*'

Slowly the note changed. Slowly the irrepressible Shaw broke through . . . . '*H.G. was no gentleman. Nobody understood better than he what gentry means; his Clissold novels prove this beyond question. But he could not or would not act the part . . . .*

'*. . . he himself became entirely classless; for though 'Erbert Wells had become H. G. Wells esquire he never behaved like a gentleman —nor like a shop assistant, nor like a schoolmaster, nor like anyone on earth but himself. And what a charmer he was . . . .*'[1]

In one category Shaw could place him with absolute certainty: he was the most completely spoilt child he had known, since even Lord Alfred Douglas had borne criticism in the form of an Eton flogging, at least once. People regarded Wells' youth as the struggle of genius to overcome poverty and hardship. This was nonsense. It was one sweet ascent '*from the foot of the ladder to the top without a single failure or check*'. There were no gaps in his meals, he never wore seedy clothes, he was never unemployed '*and always indulged as more or less an infant prodigy*'.

Shaw said he had to write and have rejected five novels over nine years while Wells was declared a genius when he had

[1] *New Statesman*, 1946.

written one short story. Quickly pampered '*into becoming the most sensitive plant in the literary greenhouse*', H.G. was brought to a state where '*the faintest shadow of disapproval threw him into transports of vituperative fury in which he would not spare his most devoted friends*'.

Yet, Shaw concluded, H.G. had not an enemy on earth. All these tantrums, this flying into rages, did not deceive his friends. His attacks were quite without malice. He simply '*warned people that he went on like that*' Shaw wrote '*and they really must try not to mind*'. Nothing, in the end, could destroy his likeableness.

Shaw had reached his ninetieth year when he wrote this obituary. He remained the same inveterate dealer in paradox prepared to assert his own laws in place of those of nature, and if it was wit in his bloodstream which kept the pulses beating long beyond the normal span, sheer physical vigour made it seem impossible that such an upright carriage, gleaming eye and brilliant tongue could ever admit the commonplace process of decay and death. Death knocked continuously and went away unanswered, but at last one day the knocking continued. A strange thing happened then. H. G. Wells came to life again. He came to life in the form of an 'obituary' of Shaw which Wells had written some time before his own death.[1] It said:

'*I have known G.B.S. intimately since I was, for a brief interval, dramatic critic for Harry Cust's* Pall Mall Gazette *half a century ago. . . . . Later on he taught me how to listen to music by insisting that I get a pianola. . . . But between the dramatic criticism and the pianola there was a long interval, and we had come to a very close friendly antagonism, an endless bickering of essentially antagonistic natures . . .*'

Shaw's excitement in life, Wells said, came from rousing a fury of antagonism which he immediately overcame, and Wells regarded him as unsurpassed at this game which occupied far too much of his life. It was, however, a small fault beside his vanity. '*Shaw was fantastically vain. He was ruled by a*

[1] *Daily Express*, November 3, 1950. H. G. Wells.

naked, unqualified, egocentric, devouring vanity, such as one rarely meets in life.'

Supremely oblivious to the streak of vanity in his own make-up Wells went on to ask—what precisely was this egotism, this vanity? Was it innate? Had it careful cultivation? It most expressed itself in Shaw's inability to think of any distinguished human being without at once drawing comparisons with himself. Wells continued . . .'*Shakespeare is manifestly a synthesis of a group of collaborators, of whom one in particular had a turn for happy language and poetic creations, but Shaw fell into the trap that identifies the author of* Coriolanus *with the poet of* A Midsummer Night's Dream *and found in the collected result a formidable rival who had to be mastered and superseded.'*

Another method of self assertion had made it difficult for Wells to travel anywhere in Europe without stumbling upon a bust or portrait of Shaw. '*The number of pictures, busts, portraits that cumbered Shaw's establishment was extraordinary. I used to imagine some great convulsion of nature making a new Herculaneum of London. As one art treasure was disinterred after another, the world would come to believe that for a time London was populated entirely by a race of men with a strong physical likeness to the early Etruscans—men with potato noses and a flamboyant bearing.'*[1]

There followed the story of the death of Wells' wife. Shaw's protestations that there was no such thing as cancer had hurt Wells badly. He was, he said, always grateful for the intervention of Charlotte, Shaw's wife . . . '*Dear Charlotte! Shaw wept bitterly when she died; he went about London weeping. Shaw drank that cup to the dregs—and then seemed to forget about it. That is the way with us ageing men. In the decay of our minds the later acquisitions go first. . . . I had no desire to see him now that Charlotte had gone and after one encounter I avoided him.'*

As the obituary drew to a close, the old irony came back. '*He is one of those minds to which money is real and not merely a counter in a game, and I shall not be surprised to find that he has*

[1] *Daily Express,* November 3, 1950. H. G. Wells.

devised his very considerable accumulations to a National Theatre
that will glorify—Shakespeare-Shaw?'

The voices were quiet at last. The grandiloquent debate lived
on. Whatever niceties of modern thinking have superseded
their respective views, there is no one today to take the place
they filled in quite the same manner. Scientists regard Shaw's
Life Force as the affectation of a literary man; politicians, Wells'
World Government as burking the issue of how to achieve it;
philosophers, both their systems of thought as verbal confusions; but their influence on the thinking of the masses in their
day and age was greater than the combined force of scientist—
politician—philosopher, and it would be false to judge them as
any one of these. They were writers, expositors, creative artists and magnificently forced the birth of the modern men-
tality. What they said varied between the romantic and the
profound, the naïve and the highly original, but the clash of
personalities capable of verbal annihilation in the grand manner was part of an age which has vanished—or do I hear the
echo of dead voices stirring at quite such a challenge?

Select Bibliography

Some fifty unpublished letters have been used or consulted apart from many books and pamphlets including:

G. K. Chesterton	*Alarms and Discussions*	Methuen & Co.
G. K. Chesterton	*George Bernard Shaw*	The Bodley Head
G. K. Chesterton	*Do We Agree?*	Cecil Palmer
G. K. Chesterton and G. G. Coulton	*The Superstitions of a Sceptic*	W. Heffer
M. Ward	*G. K. Chesterton*	Sheed and Ward
G. G. Coulton	*Mr Hilaire Belloc as Historian*	
Hilaire Belloc	*The Case of Dr Coulton*	Sheed and Ward
J. B. Morton	*Hilaire Belloc*	Hollis and Carter
G. G. Coulton	*Fourscore Years*	Cambridge University Press
Sarah Campion	*Father: A Portrait of G. G. Coulton*	Michael Joseph
Bernard Shaw	*Pen Portraits and Reviews*	Constable
Hesketh Pearson	*Life and Personality of Bernard Shaw*	Collins
James Sutherland	*Oxford Book of English Talk*	O.U.P.
Blanche Patch	*Thirty Years with G.B.S.*	Gollancz
Archibald Henderson	*Bernard Shaw, Playboy and Prophet*	D. Appleton & Co.
H. G. Wells	*Experiment in Autobiography*	Gollancz and Cresset Press
Vincent Brome	*H. G. Wells*	Longmans, Green
Doris Jones	*Life and Letters of Henry A. Jones*	Gollancz
Henry James	*Henry James and Robert Louis Stevenson*	Rupert Hart-Davis
Michael Swan	*Henry James*	Arthur Barker
Henry James	*The Letters of Henry James Selected and edited by Percy Lubbock*	Macmillan & Co. Ltd.
Edited Simon Nowell-Smith	*The Legend of the Master*	Constable
L. Edel	*Henry James*	Rupert Hart-Davis
Henry James	*The Art of Fiction*	Oxford University Press

Lytton Strachey	*Queen Victoria*	Chatto and Windus
The Stalin-Wells Talk	Pamphlet	*New Statesman*
H. G. Wells	*Mr Belloc Objects*	A. C. Watt
Hilaire Belloc	*A Companion to Mr Wells' Outline of History*	Sheed and Ward
Hilaire Belloc	*Mr Belloc Still Objects*	Sheed and Ward
Maisie Ward	*Gilbert Keith Chesterton*	Sheed and Ward
H. G. Wells	*The Conquest of Time*	A. C. Watts
H. A. Jones	*My Dear Wells*	Evelyn, Nash & Grayson
G. B. Shaw	*The Doctors Dilemma*	Constable
H. G. Wells	*Russia in the Shadows*	Hodder & Stoughton

PRIVATELY PRINTED PAMPHLETS

H. A. Jones	*Mr Mayor of Shakespeare's Town*	
G. G. Coulton	*Divorce, Mr Belloc and the Daily Telegraph*	Barnicotts
G. B. Shaw	*The Future of Religion*	
G. K. Chesterton	*Replies to Mr Shaw*	
Edited by G. H. Bowker	*Shaw on Vivisection*	National Anti-Vivisection Society

Among many newspaper and periodical files examined were the following:

The Review of the Churches, The Daily Mail, The Sunday Express, The Sunday Chronicle, Granta, The New Age, The Catholic Universe, The Dublin Review, The Nation, The Daily Telegraph, The New Statesman and Nation, The Daily Chronicle.